AUSTRALIAN
WINES

Jeni Port is a Melbourne-based wine writer
with the *Age* newspaper. She also contributes
regularly to various wine magazines. She has
broadcast on wine and is a past president of
the Wine Press Club of Australia.

CHOOSING
AUSTRALIAN
WINES

JENI PORT

A BUYER'S GUIDE

PENGUIN BOOKS

Penguin Books Australia Ltd
487 Maroondah Highway, PO Box 257
Ringwood, Victoria 3134, Australia
Penguin Books Ltd
Harmondsworth, Middlesex, England
Penguin Putnam Inc.
375 Hudson Street, New York, New York 10014, USA
Penguin Books Canada Limited
10 Alcorn Avenue, Toronto, Ontario, Canada M4V 3B2
Penguin Books (NZ) Ltd
Cnr Rosedale and Airborne Roads, Albany, Auckland, New Zealand
Penguin Books (South Africa) (Pty) Ltd
4 Pallinghurst Road, Parktown 2193, South Africa

First published by Penguin Books Australia Ltd 1992
This revised and updated edition published 1997

10 9 8 7 6 5 4

Typeset in Cheltenham Light Condensed by Midland Typesetters,
Maryborough, Victoria
Printed in Australia by Australian Print Group, Maryborough, Victoria

National Library of Australia
Cataloguing-in-Publication data:

Port, Jeni.
  Choosing Australian wines : a buyers guide.

  Rev. and updated ed.
  ISBN 0 14 026727 1.

  1. Wine and wine making – Australia. 2. Wineries –
Australia. I. Title. (Series : Penguin pocket series).

641.220994

CONTENTS

INTRODUCTION

For a nation of beer drinkers we drink a lot of wine. It is sometimes forgotten that while Australians are among the world's heartiest drinkers of beer, we are also the biggest consumers of wine among English-speaking nations. Each year we drink around 18 litres of wine per head. The majority is grown and produced right here; in fact every State and Territory – even the Northern Territory – has vineyards.

The subject of Australian wine may seem broad and bewildering because at any one time we have more than 15 000 wine labels for sale, covering different styles, different vintages or years and very different markets. The average consumer new to wine may not feel very confident choosing wine. Now in its third edition, this guide, a primer for the budding enthusiast, is aimed at explaining what the average consumer needs to know.

We start with wine styles and an explanation of why some wines should be named after the grape (or grapes) contained in the bottle and why some are not. This is a story that dates from the arrival of the first European settlers and lays the groundwork for the following chapters on the new as well as the more established grape varieties grown in Australia today.

Why is chardonnay so popular today? What were the reasons behind the downfall of the riesling grape and what can we expect in the way of future trends?

The king of red grapes – cabernet sauvignon – has evolved into a sophisticated international wine style, while a grape with a much longer history in this country, shiraz, has finally excited not only Australian drinkers but wine lovers from the United States to the United Kingdom. Why? And where can the best examples of these (as well as many other wines) be found in Australia today?

Australia's major contribution to the international wine scene, a unique fortified wine tradition of ports and liqueur muscats, is also covered.

Readers will find some practical drinking advice on good Australian wines to buy and try under the 'And now to taste' sections. (For this third edition, the wines listed are as current as possible. At the time of going to press, many 1996 whites were coming on to the market, as well as some 1994 reds.) Chapter 5 offers help in deciphering the often confusing language of the winemaker and the wine taster.

While some may profit from treating wine as something mysterious, only revealing itself to a few, the truth is that wine is an everyday drink that, while quite enticing in its mystery, can be enjoyed by everybody.

Learning more about its many facets will not necessarily make wine taste any better, but *Choosing Australian Wines* will help readers seek out and taste Australian wine in its many various and wonderful guises.

As return readers to the book will note, the Australian wine industry has not been standing still these last two years between editions.

Price rises and the breaking of the $10-a-bottle barrier that previously existed for good, everyday drinking wines has been a constant talking point and source of pain in the wallet. (In response to this, we have changed the price ranges in the 'And Now to Taste' sections in this book accordingly.) What was once an enjoyable drink at $10 a bottle now fetches $12 or more. In one case, a Victorian sparkling wine went from $17 to $25 in one incredible leap. The maker thought it was worth the hike. At least one wine retailer refused to sell it.

To say that the industry is in a state of flux is to state the obvious. The escalating growth in sales of Australian wines overseas has brought its own pressures on price and supply. Unfortunately for domestic drinkers, overseas wine drinkers crave exactly the same kind of wines: that is, dry table wines made from premium grape varieties. Something has to give, and it is not just price. There is a nagging feeling that Australian wine drinkers are helping subsidise export sales through higher prices here.

The answer for the industry has been to plant more vines and establish more vineyards. The past five years have seen huge tracts of land across the nation given over to vines. Cape Jaffa, near Robe on the South Australian coast, and Perth Hills are just two new viticultural regions to have been established. In the record 1998 vintage (when around 950 000 tonnes were harvested) we saw some of the results of those early plantings, and with each successive vintage we will see more and more wine coming on stream. However, it is doubtful whether price drops will accompany this increased supply. It will be used to satiate export demand – while it lasts.

Export has been good for the industry, and not always in a way obvious to the consumer. It has been responsible, in part, for a new look being taken at the age-old problem of cork taint. For years, winemakers have grumbled about but accepted cork taint, where microscopic moulds growing in the cork come in contact with the wine and spoil it. The general feeling was that although cork taint was spoiling up to 5 per cent of wines there was no way around the problem as few could see an acceptable alternative to the traditional cork sourced from the cork tree.

With the popularity of Australian wines overseas it could be argued that winemakers have finally been given an incentive to act. The reputation of Australian wine is at stake. Some companies are seeking out the Stelvin screw-cap closure once more (a near-perfect closure used in the 1970s and then dropped because of its unattractive look). Others are moving into synthetic closures that look the part and that are impervious to microscopic moulds.

This new edition of *Choosing Australian Wines* arrives at a time of exciting change in the Australian wine industry. But wherever the future takes us, may we all be assured of drinking well and always in moderation.

AND NOW TO TASTE

The 'And now to taste' sections of the book list Australian wines made from the different grape varieties. They fall into three price categories.

$$$

($15 and upwards per bottle)

$$

(between $10 and $15 per bottle)

$

(up to $10 per bottle)

Smaller than expected vintages in the early 1990s and growing international demand for Australian wines have resulted in substantial price rises, especially in red wines, where the demand is greatest. Please note that the prices mentioned can differ from store to store and State to State. This is a guide only.

WINE STYLES

Once your interest is aroused, learning more about different wine styles is a highly enjoyable pastime. The most obvious starting point is to visit the many vineyards that dot the country and get first-hand knowledge from the people who make the wine (see Chapter 6). A tour and tasting will instil not only an appreciation of the product but also of the time-consuming practices that bring it to our table.

Another good way to learn more about what you drink and the various wine styles is to seek out an interested wine merchant or bottle-shop manager for advice and tastings. It is now common practice for bottle shops to put on tastings of wine and quite often they invite the winemakers to discuss their wines with customers.

The third way is to read as much as you can on the subject. Many newspapers and magazines now have wine columns that write up new releases and interesting people and events. In addition, there are some excellent Australian publications on wine.

GENERIC VERSUS VARIETAL

The words 'generic' and 'varietal' are perhaps the two most important keys to understanding Australian wine today. They tell us what we can expect from a wine and what it is likely to taste like, and they give us the information with which to make judgements, like matching wine with the right food or occasion.

Generic wine styles

Australia has had a strong tradition of using generic descriptions of wines. The term 'generic' can be classified in a number of ways:

- the naming of wines with familiar British and European terms, generally after well-known wine regions, for example, Sauternes and Moselle
- the naming of wines after geographical locations like Champagne, Chablis, Burgundy, Beaujolais and Bordeaux, ostensibly as an aid to the consumer with regard to the style of wine
- the naming of wines after British (nongeographical) terms like claret and hock as a popular means of describing the wine in just one word. Australia, being a British colony, has used these now familiar bywords for many years
- generic also applies to popular wines made to a style, or a formula, usually from a number of grape varieties and a number of vineyard areas. Some recent examples are Lindemans Ben Ean moselle, Cawarra claret and Orlando Coolabah riesling.

The Australian wine industry has entered into a trade agreement with the European Union that will see the gradual removal of generic names like Champagne, Chablis, Sauternes and so on from Australian wine labels. Some companies are already phasing out such names.

Varietal wine styles

A relatively recent phenomenon, the use of varietal terms on wine labels and in wine writing is now favoured over generic description. 'Varietal' means naming wines after the grape varieties from which they are made. For example, cabernet sauvignon, chardonnay, riesling, and chenin blanc are all top-selling wine styles today as well as being grape varieties.

Of all the many grape varieties grown in Australia, only a relatively few produce wine with strong, individual varietal character. It is these that are usually earmarked for the buyer's attention by having their name on the label. Others, like sultana, gordo blanco and trebbiano, are used in the important cask wine and cheap commercial wine markets but are never marketed under their own names.

According to law, for an Australian wine to be labelled under its varietal name, for example, cabernet sauvignon, the wine has to contain at least 85 per cent of that particular grape. It is also allowed to have up to 15 per cent of another grape (quite commonly shiraz or merlot in the case of cabernet sauvignon). While the makers do not have to proclaim the additional grape/s on the label, they often do. However, should a wine be made up of a number of components, none of which forms a majority (85 per cent), then the grape varieties are generally listed on the label in descending order of percentage in the blend, for example, cabernet sauvignon, merlot, cabernet franc, malbec.

The word 'varietal' often pops up in tasting terms and in wine writing and is used to describe the character of a wine as derived from the grape used. For example, 'that sauvignon blanc has a strong varietal character' refers to that grape's quite marked herbaceous flavour.

WHITE GENERIC STYLES

Chablis

The name 'chablis' on Australian wine labels is used very loosely indeed, covering a wide variety of wine styles.

In France, in the small village of Chablis, in northern Burgundy, chablis is made from chardonnay. It is dry, high in acid, sees little wood treatment and is remarkably austere.

In Australia, chablis has been made from many grape varieties, with semillon a favourite, and has often been full-bodied and showing wood maturation. The Australian 'chablis' is about to become part of history now that generic names are to be phased out.

Champagne

In the early days winemakers making champagne chose grape varieties that were available – like riesling, ondenc and sultana – and manufactured the bubbles in large pressure tanks. Today many so-called Australian champagnes continue to be made in this way.

Since the 1970s winemakers have attempted to emulate true champagne production using varieties like chardonnay and pinot noir and they have fermented the wine in the bottle, which gives a smaller bubble and finer appearance and taste. Some companies have joined with the French to produce premium sparkling wines like Croser, Domaine Chandon and Yalumba D, but these wines never feature the term 'champagne' on the label. The terms 'méthode champenoise' and 'methode traditionnelle', which indicate that the true champagne method has been used, are now often preferred.

Moselle

Once all the rage, thanks largely to the phenomenal success of Ben Ean moselle in the 1970s, moselle now keeps a much quieter profile. It led the white wine boom, later shared by its sister brand Liebfrauwine, but these wines bore little resemblance to their typical Geman namesakes found on the Mosel River in Germany.

Riesling

Decades of confusion over the name 'riesling' have resulted in riesling becoming a generic. Its use has usually indicated a semi-sweet wine. The words 'rhine riesling' were used to help overcome the confusion and denote the real thing, but in truth the grape's correct name is riesling (see Chapter 2).

Sauternes

Sauternes, a wine district in Bordeaux in southwestern France, produces some of the most luscious and expensive sweet dessert wines in the world. Chateau d'Yquem is its most famous winemaking house employing the most time-consuming methods, including the picking of individual berries that have been affected by the botrytis mould, which is the secret of great sauternes.

In Australia, these methods have been far too expensive to even consider, so for years fortified wine has been added to a dry white wine to produce Australian sauternes. Botrytis is very much a hit-and-miss proposition here, depending almost entirely on climate, but some companies have worked at encouraging it in the vineyard. De Bortoli makes a bold effort at authenticity using the semillon grape, and there are those who make similarly fine wines. However, obliged by an international agreement to phase out the name 'sauternes', producers are favouring the terms 'noble riesling' or 'botrytised riesling' or even a new name altogether, such as De Bortoli's Noble One.

White burgundy

White burgundy, as we know it, came into being in 1936 when Western Australian winemaker the late Jack Mann made his first Houghton's white burgundy, a big, full-flavoured white wine made from chenin blanc grapes. When the wine finally arrived in the eastern States in the 1950s it was an immediate hit, sparking a rash of inevitable look-alikes. But white burgundy soon lost its way, for while technically well made the wines were eventually roundly criticised for lacking real flavour; mere skeletons of acid and sugar. Popular grapes were semillon and chenin blanc but in France chardonnay is the grape from which all great white burgundy is made. There really is no comparison and soon Australian companies will no longer be allowed to use 'burgundy' on their labels.

RED GENERIC STYLES

Burgundy
Just as Australian winemakers came to make their own version of claret (Bordeaux-style red), they decided by a similar twist of logic that burgundy was a heavier wine than claret but otherwise not greatly different! In fact, in some vineyards the free-run wine (the first and best juice from the grapes, which flows without hard pressing) was sold as claret, and the pressed wine with its greater body and extracted flavour was sold as burgundy. It was even thought that young clarets would eventually, with bottle ageing, soften and become full-bodied burgundy. Admittedly, all of this was before pinot noir (the real French burgundy red grape) was available in Australia.

Claret
'Claret' is an English term picked up for use in Australia that at various times has come to mean a dry red supposedly similar to those from Bordeaux in France. The red wines of Bordeaux, rich in tannin and slow to mature, derive their distinctive flavour and bouquet from the cabernet sauvignon grape. Early on, cabernet sauvignon was not freely available in Australia and makers substituted shiraz in its place or a blend of shiraz and mataro. Some excellent wines were made

under the Moyston, St Henri, Jacob's Creek and Redman labels but the name is rarely seen today.

Madeira

Originally from the island of the same name off the coast of Morocco in the Atlantic Ocean, madeira is made by the solera system (also used in making sherry, see Chapter 4) and employs four specific grape varieties, which Australian winemakers do not use. Today few persist with the wine, the style having gone out of fashion and trade agreements restricting the use of the term 'madeira'.

Port

Port is a fortified dessert wine produced in Portugal. It is grown on the steep slopes along the banks of the Douro River and can be made from a variety of grapes, some of which are also grown in Australia. However, much Australian port continues to be made from grenache, shiraz, mataro and cabernet sauvignon with very different results. Australian ports are generally heavier in appearance and sweeter than those of Portugal. Australian vintage ports (from a single year) are more highly extracted, contain more tannin and colour and are more robust. We do make some fine ports that compare quite favourably with those from Portugal, but in the coming years Australian producers will have to find another name to call their wine. Having agreed that Portugal has the right to the name, some are already emphasising the words 'tawny' and 'vintage' as substitutes on labels.

Sherry

Sherry is well known in Australia and has become an integral part of the wine industry, but the name derives from the renowned fortified wines of the Andalusia region of Spain. Production, centring around the city of Jerez (pronounced hare-eth), is strictly controlled by government legislation. No such regulation occurs in Australia, but Australian winemakers have been anxious to at least employ traditional sherry grapes – palomino and pedro ximinez – and winemaking techniques, which is not the case with some other generic styles. This attention to detail has paid off with some fine wines being made, but, like the names port and madeira, Australian producers will have to find another description for their wine in the future.

RIESLING

A true classic grape variety, riesling is at home in Germany but has managed to find considerable success in Australia. Although widely planted, it is most suited to the relatively cool climes of southern Western Australia, South Australia, Victoria and Tasmania. At its best it is dry and as crisp as a fresh apple, fruity with a hint of aromatics (flowery and spicy) and has a deep, lingering flavour.

However, as we shall see there is confusion concerning its true name and whether the term 'rhine riesling' should be dropped in favour of just 'riesling'. This confusion will soon be settled when Australia and the European Union have settled on a phasing-out period for the prefix 'rhine', which has deliberate European connotations. In keeping with that move, the term 'riesling' is used throughout this chapter for simplicity's sake.

What's in a name?

Riesling showed an early aptitude in Australian conditions, being planted by the enterprising Macarthur family at Camden, New South Wales, in 1838. Reports of the time had the resulting wine the best in the colonies. A fellow compatriot James King settled in the viticulturally awakening Hunter

Valley and did particularly well with Shepherd's riesling. It later underwent a name change to Hunter River riesling and flourished there, but the truth always remained that the grape was in fact semillon.

In South Australia, the strong German community was responsible for the import of what was then believed to be riesling. As the German winemakers came from Silesia, an area not known for its wine, it is not surprising that what then became known for years as Clare riesling was in fact a grape variety called crouchen!

Some time later in the 1800s, riesling figured prominently in the much-vaunted whites of the old Lilydale vineyards in Victoria's Yarra Valley.

Despite the hit-and-miss approach, enthusiasm for riesling was fuelled by these early successes. But it was only after we had had our fill of fortified wine (the main taste of the 1950s) and then red (the 1960s) that we turned our attention to white wine and to riesling (the 1970s).

Advances in white-winemaking technology like temperature control of fermentation (the process of converting sugar in grapes into alcohol) were well suited to capturing riesling's delicate, aromatic properties, producing crisp, fresh wines of a quality that could not be ignored.

And then, of course, there was the advent and eventual wine-market domination of the wine cask, which contributed in no small way to per capita consumption jumping from 8.8 litres in 1970–71 to 17.3 litres in 1979–80. The white boom and riesling had arrived!

A popular drink

The beauty of a grape like riesling is its versatility. Clean and fresh when young, it can also mature into a wine of many interesting bottle-developed flavours with time. It has been made into sparkling wine, is ideal as a sweet dessert wine and has even been used in the making of fortifieds. But it is as a young wine that most of us enjoy it today.

The person widely held responsible for showing producers the way towards increased riesling drinkability – the creator of today's popular style – is Brian Croser.

The year was 1975. The place was Thomas Hardy and Sons, McLaren Vale, South Australia, where Croser was winemaker. The wine was a Siegersdorf 'rhine riesling'. Croser inaugurated a new style for Australia by leaving a little natural grape sugar (called residual sugar) in the finished wine. The sugar provided a smooth roundness to the wine, complementing its fresh and highly delicate fruitiness. This was the catalyst for a rash of lookalikes that attracted widespread acceptance, and, within a number of years, criticism. The trouble was that in their enthusiasm many winemakers produced a palatable but boring mediocrity in so many rieslings that the difference between good and bad became negligible. Residual sugar was also good at hiding faults.

The new technology used was also criticised for making riesling too clean and too delicate. Fruit character became just a passing sniff in the glass. Sales started to tumble during the 1980s as consumers eyed the full-flavoured newcomer, chardonnay.

The return of riesling to the drinker's good books has been slow, but a number of producers have sought to persevere with highly individual styles of riesling. Others have learnt from their early mistakes. Indeed, the grape has much in its favour. It does not require the enormous expense of new wood as many chardonnays do, and is still the second most widely planted classic white grape variety in Australia, so its retail price remains highly attractive.

Riesling or rhine riesling?

Early confusion over riesling's identity has led to the wine industry's use of the classic grape variety as a generic wine style. This unique situation arose after a series of historical mishaps that saw grapes such as crouchen and semillon mistakenly named Clare riesling and Hunter River riesling. The term 'rhine riesling' was introduced to help separate the real thing from the bogus copies that had already gained popularity under their assumed names. Unfortunately, the damage had been done.

An industry body, the Australian Wine and Brandy Producers' Association, declared early on that 'riesling' could be both a varietal and a generic term, basing its opinion on records that confirmed the use of 'riesling' as a generic term dating back to the early 1860s. You may ask what's in a name, but definition becomes important when a customer can pay good money for a 'riesling' that may not contain any rhine riesling at all. A generic term, after all, indicates a wine style rather than a specific grape variety.

An increasing number of winemakers are dropping the prefix 'rhine' in favour of just 'riesling', the wine's true name, pre-empting Australian–European Union trade talks on the phasing out of popular wine names like rhine riesling and lambrusco. However, confusion in the marketplace abounds. Rest assured that the name 'riesling' on wines from the likes of Mountadam (Adelaide Hills), Knights (Macedon), Pipers Brook (Tasmania), Tim Adams (Clare Valley) and others indicates not only the real thing but the winemakers' willingness to get the name right.

A little rot

One riesling that can be bought with the utmost confidence is the limited and highly desirable botrytised riesling, a sweet dessert wine generally of the highest quality. Its concentrated richness and complexity is such that only a small glassful is enough at any one time.

The secret to this under-rated Australian wine is a mould or rot called *Botrytis cinerea*, which requires wet, humid conditions in the vineyard to grow and attach itself to the already ripened grapes. Winemakers are very much in the hands of the gods when it comes to botrytis, and should the wet and humid weather continue, the grapes will simply split and become spoilt. However, if all goes well the botrytis spores germinate forming a highly unattractive blue-grey film on the grapes, which effectively removes water and concentrates the sugar, grape and botrytis flavours in the now shrivelled grape.

The botrytis infection imparts a special flavour of its own that is highly prized and is often, not surprisingly, referred to as 'noble rot'.

This 'noble' taste is reflected in the great sweet wines of the world – the Sauternes and Barsac wines of France, Germany's beerenauslese and trockenbeerenauslese and Hungarian tokay. In Australia, some arresting sweet styles using riesling are made by Brown Brothers (noble riesling), Tollana, Petaluma, Mitchelton (botrytis-affected rhine riesling), Heggies (botrytis-affected, late-harvest rhine riesling) and Hardy's.

Modern technology has also enabled winemakers whose vineyards were previously not climatically disposed to botrytis to spray grapes with botrytis spores and let them do their work in temperature- and humidity-controlled storerooms. Primo Estate in the Adelaide Plains has enjoyed great success with its innoculation methods.

Most good botrytis rieslings are rich and viscous, golden in colour with a taste of sweet honey and apricot. A well-balanced wine needs acid to prevent cloying and can be lightly chilled, especially in warmer months. It is first and foremost a dessert wine, being especially delicious with fruit-based finales such as summer pudding and fruit tarts as well as the more traditional crème caramel or gâteaux.

Riesling is also used extensively in the making of sweet wines that have not been affected by the botrytis mould. In the past, winemakers relied on three German terms to explain these styles to the drinking public. Today, they are not quite as common as they were (and have been listed for phasing out in future Australia–European Union trade discussions). They are:

- **spätlese.**   In German the word refers to late harvest, which means the grapes were left a little longer than usual on the vine to become fully ripe and sweet. This wine is simple and sweet.

- **auslese.**   In German the word refers to selected late-harvested grapes. That selection process generally implies a wine of higher quality than the spätlese. Botrytis may or may not be involved.

- **beerenauslese** and **trockenbeerenauslese.**   These are German terms for wines made from individually selected ripe grapes that have become partially dried or raisined. These wines are generally of the highest quality possible, rich in luscious fruit taste and worthy of ageing. Botrytis is often involved in their making.

And now to taste

The following is a selection of Australian wines made from the riesling grape variety.

$$$

- **Leconfield 12 Row Riesling (1996)**
  Riesling in Coonawarra is increasingly being grubbed out in favour of red grape varieties. This particular wine is

among the last of its breed. Pity, because it is extremely easy drinking – its full citrus flavour is sharpened by a clean acid backbone.

- **Leydens Vale Riesling (1994)**
A bottle-aged riesling released late 1996 that illustrates the changes this grape undergoes with time. It is starting to develop more toasty characters and is quite full-bodied, oily in texture and aromatic to the taste. The fruit was sourced from the Yarra Valley and Mount Barker.

- **Petaluma Riesling (1996)**
It is easy to appreciate why this wine from the Adelaide Hills is among the most expensive rieslings in Australia. First impact comes from the scent of lemons and sweet floral aromatics. But it is the depth of flavour and its persistence in the mouth that really impresses. This wine ages beautifully too.

- **Seppelt Drumborg Vineyard Riesling (1996)**
Drumborg was developed in south-west Victoria expressly for its cool climate fruit. This makes it well suited to riesling. Floral scent, almost spicy, followed by good middle palate mouthfeel and super-dry finish.

- **Tyrrell's Clare Valley Riesling (1996)**
Classic riesling characters are evident here with lemons, limes and hints of lychees on the nose followed by a rich, developed flavour. Fresh and tangy, like a good riesling always should be. The maker is Hunter-based but the grapes are from a noted South Australian riesling area.

$$

- **Galafrey Rhine Riesling (1995)**
  The Great Southern region of Western Australia may have started late with riesling but is making up for lost time with a growing reputation for impressive, concentrated wines. The Galafrey wine fits the bill with its depth of citrussy, lemony flavours and its freshness.
- **Mitchelton Blackwood Park Riesling (1996)**
  Consistently ranked as one of the best-priced and delicious rieslings in the country. It can rarely be faulted on taste, easy drinkability, price or even ageing potential. An all-round stunner from the Goulburn Valley.
- **Pike's Riesling (1996)**
  You always get great depth of flavour in a good Clare riesling. Not wishy-washy in the least. The traditional style is epitomised here in winemaker Neil Pike's baby, which shows plenty of attractive lime, lemon and spicy flavours.
- **Skillogalee Riesling (1996)**
  This Clare Valley riesling specialist produces some of the better styles in the country. Even in their youth they can show complex flavours as this wine does with its rich blend of zesty limes, lemons, aromatics and clean acid finish. Will take further ageing.
- **Tim Gramp Watervale Riesling (1996)**
  It is wines such as this one that will bring riesling back into drinkers' good books. It is simply a pure expression

of fruit with no residual sugar but plenty of citrus and spicy characters.

$

- **De Bortoli Sacred Hill Rhine Riesling (1996)**
  A well-priced riesling from the Riverina, which like many in this price range is noticeable for the level of residual sugar sweetness giving mouth-filling richness. Clear riesling character is also defined, as is a crisp, acid finish.
- **Eaglehawk Riesling (1995)**
  A medium gold colour denotes something with a little age. The flavours are fruity with a citrussy bite, and more than a pinch of residual sugar can be tasted. A simple wine meant for early drinking.
- **Miranda High Country Rhine Riesling (1995)**
  The Riverina-based Miranda company sources grapes from many different regions in order to produce distinctive varietal styles. This cool-climate Victorian wine certainly has riesling's hallmark aromatic nose and shows lively acid and lychee flavours.
- **Orlando Jacob's Creek Rhine Riesling (1996)**
  Multi-district sourcing means this style rarely changes in quality or taste from year to year. This is its strength, as is its near-perfect balance between floral and citrus flavours and mouth-cleansing crispness.

- **Peter Lehmann Eden Valley Riesling (1996)**
  A famous Barossa Valley name has sourced riesling from
  the neighbouring, higher and cooler Eden Valley for this
  wine and the pedigree shows with intense flavour and
  steely dryness.

Which food?

As riesling is a most versatile grape variety coming in both dry
and sweet forms it can be matched with a number of very different foods and courses from the start to the finish of a meal.

Pre-dinner drinks   A dry refreshing riesling to start is a
pleasant way to enter a meal.

Hors d'oeuvre   An assortment of bite-sized raw vegetables
or a more elaborate Italian antipasto selection of, for example,
salami, cold meat, olives and marinated mushrooms is an
ideal accompaniment to a full-bodied riesling.

First course   It is traditional to serve a dry white with the
first course and riesling fits the bill perfectly: baked fish,
seafood (crayfish, prawns, oysters), roast chicken, ham,
seafood-based pasta, quiche.

Main course   Generally an aged riesling or at least a full-
bodied style is suited to most main-course fare except very
rich red meats and most game: Chinese food, veal, poultry,
fish, seafood, Japanese raw fish, light curry.

Dessert   An aged or sweet or botrytis-affected riesling will suit dessert, from the sweet and savoury to the very, very sweet: soufflé, fruit tart, trifle, torte, crème caramel, fresh fruit (peaches, apricots, nectarines), nuts.

Cheese   Brie, cheddar, pecorino, ricotta and figs, camembert, fruit cheese, emmentaler.

After-dinner drinks   A rich, aged botrytised riesling.

CHARDONNAY

Irrespective of climate or terrain, chardonnay is found in every major Australian wine-growing area, from the coastal fringes of Western Australia to the dry heat of South Australia's Riverland, as far north as Queensland and as south as Tasmania's Derwent Valley. All this has happened within the space of just two decades.

Chardonnay's tremendous growth is reflected in industry statistics that show chardonnay rising from literally nowhere 20 years ago to becoming our second largest white wine grape planted (outside the multi-purpose grape sultana), with almost 15 000 hectares. Its position in France, where 13 000 hectares are planted, is similarly important.

Popularity has spread just as fast outside Australia. In 1988 the prestigious English wine magazine *Decanter* held a tasting of the 'greatest' chardonnays in the world. Of the top 10 placings, five went to Australian chardonnays with Rothbury Estate Hunter

Valley Reserve Chardonnay 1986, from New South Wales, turning in the best performance in fourth place. The judges were able to precisely pinpoint the main attraction: 'The French wines here were like the French themselves, a bit withdrawn and taking some time to get to know. The Australian wines were upfront, saying "G'day, how are you?" '.

The glamour grape

So what is it about this most fashionable and glamorous of today's grape varieties? It has a lot to do with the development and clever marketing of the grape by the French over the past 200 years or more. Although the grape originated in the Middle East, it was taken by the French who made it their own. Chardonnay is now the classic ingredient in not one but three of France's premier wines: chablis, white burgundy and champagne.

Responding to each wine region's own particular climate and each vineyard's special features (often called a mesoclimate, which encompasses a vineyard's altitude, elevation and exposure to wind, among other factors), chardonnay has produced three separate and highly attractive wine styles much copied in Australia.

At the northern outpost of Burgundy, Chablis, a harsh climate is responsible for chardonnay being high in acid with a taste that is often called steely (firm, lean, acidic). This style is opposite the opulence of chardonnay grown further south in Burgundy's Côte-d'Or and Côte de Nuits. Here, the vineyards produce naturally soft, fruit-filled wines that benefit from chardonnay's other great gift, its affinity with oak, producing great complexity with age. The wines have usually been matured, and are sometimes also fermented, in small oak barrels, with the prolonged contact imparting warm, honeyed qualities.

In the cold northern climate of Champagne it is the third and last great quality of chardonnay – its blending ability – that stands out. Here, chardonnay grows side by side with the red grape pinot noir, and side by side they remain in many a bottle of fine champagne. Blending the two grapes brings their best qualities to the finished wine: pinot noir provides the strength and structure, chardonnay brings delicacy and full, rounded flavour. Sometimes champagne is made using only chardonnay and is called blanc de blancs. Here the blender's art is just as important. By combining various parcels of wine from different vineyards and vintage years, an elegant and complex wine can be produced.

These three important lessons in learning and appreciating the beauty of chardonnay – climate, oak maturation and blending – are still being learnt and mastered in Australia today.

Determining style

With chardonnay growing in every major Australian wine region, it is climate that provides the first and most important factor in determining style and quality.

Climate

In its home (or at least where chardonnay was first claimed

to be grown commercially) in the Hunter Valley, New South Wales, chardonnay receives liberal doses of sunshine during the growing season resulting in a generally well-ripened, round and buttery style. This seems to be the same story with chardonnay grown in warmer climates like the Barossa Valley in South Australia, northeastern Victoria, Western Australia's Swan Valley and Mudgee in New South Wales. While generosity of fruit is rarely a problem, acid, or rather the lack of it, can sometimes result in a rather flabby (lacking crispness), overblown style with little finesse.

Picking times become crucial in such areas. As sugar levels (and potential alcohol) increase inside the grapes during ripening, the acid level declines. Early picking often ensures a fair degree of natural acid in the wine for a firm structure and added zip to the taste.

In hot climates, notably South Australia's Riverland and the Riverina centred on Griffith in New South Wales, chardonnay's importance tends to take a back seat to more commercially useful (and successful) grapes like doradillo and sultana, which are the basis of both regions' huge commitment to the cask wine market. The presence of the classic chardonnay grape in these areas is often criticised for producing lacklustre wines. However, with careful vine management chardonnay can perform very well in the heat. These wines are often well priced, too, and offer real value for money.

Cooler climates and their effect on classic grape varieties like chardonnay currently seem to excite the industry and consumers alike most. Long, cool growing conditions in regions like the Adelaide Hills, McLaren Vale and Padthaway (South Australia); Yarra Valley, Mornington Peninsula, Macedon (Victoria); Pipers Brook (Tasmania); and Margaret River and Mount Barker–Frankland River (Western Australia) are said to concentrate flavour and acid. While acid gives a sharp crispness to a wine, the grape's flavour is enhanced by a degree of oak maturation. The final result in the glass should be a careful balance of all three, with neither one nor the others being too conspicuous. These are the wines that should age the best and generally need to have a little more bottle maturation before drinking than a chardonnay wine from the warm to hot regions.

Winemaking

Another major contribution to the style and quality of an Australian chardonnay is the winemaking process. Unlike many white grape varieties, chardonnay is highly compatible with oak and after some time in oak can develop well-rounded and rich flavours, which many winemakers find highly desirable. The critical questions remain: which oak and for how long?

When it comes to oak there are a number of choices. The United States, France and Germany are the main suppliers of oak casks for wine, the transport of which tends to make them very expensive in Australia. French oak is by far the most popular with winemakers worldwide, with different forests – Limousin, Nevers, Troncais – giving different characters to the wood, which are transferred to the wine.

New oak barrels, or barrels that have had wine in them

for a year or two, are the most prized for quality wine because of the effect on a wine's bouquet and texture. Among its more obvious contributions are the smell of vanilla as well as sweet and spicy nuances. Tannin from new oak gives a firm, dry, complex texture that is said to bring a sharper definition to a wine, like bringing a hazy picture into focus.

How long chardonnay should remain in oak in order to savour its riches is entirely up to the winemaker. There is great debate on the subject but generally the more full-bodied a wine, the more oak ageing it can take. It is not unusual for chardonnay to mature in oak for up to 12 months.

There is no rule that says chardonnay has to have wood maturation, and a number of Australian winemakers have been experimenting with non-wooded chardonnay. In this case, the wine often retains delicate fruit flavours (which can be masked by oak in a young wooded chardonnay) and is cheaper to produce.

And now to taste
The following is a selection of Australian wines made from the chardonnay grape variety.

$$$

- **Cassegrain Fromenteau Reserve Chardonnay (1995)**
  This wine hails from Port Macquarie and the style is

full-on chardonnay with a strong oak component. The smell of butterscotch, cinnamon, spicy marzipan and honey is largely oak-derived, as is the lees-y, rich buttery flavour.

- **Coldstream Hills Reserve Chardonnay (1995)**
  The Yarra Valley does great chardonnay. Witness the multifaceted flavours and smells from citrus fruit to pears and figs in this wine. Stylish oak handling (cashews, cinnamon and butterscotch) completes a fine wine. All it needs is a little more ageing.

- **Eileen Hardy Chardonnay (1995)**
  The best chardonnay of each vintage is selected for this label and it shows. Grapes from the Yarra Valley and Adelaide Hills produce a reserved, fruit-driven style with marmalade, oak fermentation flavours. A wine to age.

- **Pipers Brook Vineyard Chardonnay (1995)**
  One of Tasmania's premier winemakers, Pipersbrook consistently produces a complex chardonnay combining excellent fruit and integrated oak. Note the quinces, figs and vanillan oak on the nose as well as some spicy notes and more citrus – lemons and grapefruit – following on the palate.

- **Rosemount Estate Show Reserve Chardonnay (1995)**
  The archetypal buttery chardonnay from the Hunter Valley. Super-ripe grapes and extended barrel maturation have produced a warm, seductive chardonnay flavour and feel. Especially approachable in its youth.

$$

- **Cranswick Estate Unoaked Chardonnay (1996)**
  Unwooded, unoaked – they mean the same, but these new styles don't all taste the same. This wine from the Riverina shows the characteristics of a warmer region: passionfruit, peaches, pears and bananas. A fruit salad of the nicest sort with a touch of sweetness.
- **Hardy's Sir James Chardonnay (1995)**
  The first Sir James chardonnay sees the influence of a marriage made in oak. Barrel ferment influences in the form of butterscotch dominate the nose, and there is more on the palate hiding some very attractive fruit. Give it time.
- **Oakland Unwooded Chardonnay (1996)**
  Unwooded chardonnay should provide a clear expression of fruit. This wine fits the bill with a light, tropical fruit aroma and subtle citrus flavours highlighted by a clean acidic freshness. Drink now.
- **Plunkett's Blackwood Ridge Unwooded Chardonnay (1996)**
  The high, cool Strathbogie Ranges in central Victoria has delivered tasty grapefruit, apple and pear flavours and smells to this enticing wine. Sweet fruit ripeness gives strength to the middle palate. Enjoy now.
- **Rouge Homme Coonawarra Unoaked Chardonnay (1996)**
  A delicately flavoured wine that requires minimal chilling, this unoaked chardonnay has all the shades of its cooler

climate home: grapefruit, green apple, lemons, acid. Its appley freshness will win you over.

$

- **Banrock Station Unwooded Chardonnay (1996)**
  A new label featuring Riverland fruit that is aimed at the cost-conscious. The flavour is big and mouthfilling and is fruit-driven in style with just a touch of sweetness. Drink now.
- **Deakin Estate Chardonnay (1996)**
  Another warm-area chardonnay, this time from northwest Victoria on the Murray River, and doesn't it show in the alcohol – a whopping 14 per cent! A fruit salad of pineapple and passionfruit with little oak showing, this wine is intended for early consumption.
- **Mildara Chardonnay (1996)**
  Those wondering what a buttery chardonnay smells like need go no further. This is it – melting butter on the nose is typical of oaked chardonnay, as is the ripe melons, peaches and pineapple flavour.
- **Orlando Jacob's Creek Chardonnay (1996)**
  This style helped cement Australia's reputation overseas for producing wines tasting like 'sunshine in a bottle'. It explodes with a cocktail of ripe tropical fruit smells and flavours. Rich and full-flavoured but not blowsy. A total joy.
- **Seppelt Moyston Unoaked Chardonnay (1996)**
  A subtle wine from Great Western, so do not expect to

be bowled over by a strong chardonnay flavour or feel.
The emphasis is on drinkability with delicate fruitiness
balanced by acidic freshness.

Which food?

The best chardonnays display a number of characteristics in
well-balanced proportions – a pleasing dryness, mellowness
and gentle wood maturation flavours. Foods displaying similar
flavours seem to suit the grape variety best.

Pre-dinner drinks   Chardonnay is now found in many sparkling wines (méthode champenoise) under the French term
'blanc de blancs', and is very appetising with or without food.

Hors d'oeuvre   Italian antipasto, smoked fish, chicken pâté.

First course   Australian chardonnay is made for seafood
and, in particular, shellfish such as crayfish, oysters and crab.
Creamed vegetable soup and vegetable dishes also make a
good pairing.

Main course   It is well worth remembering that most full-
bodied chardonnays can stand up to most rich meat dishes:
roast pork, chicken breasts with rich sauces, veal, cold smoked
meats, Chinese food, fish and seafood. A good wood-aged
chardonnay goes well with roast beef and grilled steak.

Cheese   Edam, gruyère (a cheese not too strong in flavour).

SEMILLON

After more than 150 years of continuous and devoted service to the Australian wine drinker, one wine that can carry the distinction of being a true 'classic' is semillon: or perhaps that should read 'Hunter River riesling', 'Shepherd's riesling', 'Large riesling' or 'Barnawartha pinot', for these have been some of the stranger names semillon has had to wear during its time here.

The confusion over name is not restricted to semillon of course, but it does seem that the native French grape variety has undergone more of an identity crisis than most. It would appear to date back to the 1830s and a collection of vines presented to the administrators of the Sydney colony for propagation and distribution. Called the Busby Collection, after the colonial viticulturist (vine grower) James Busby who chose them from the vineyards of France and Spain, it was the basis of much of the Australian wine industry as well as the source of much confusion. Established at the Botanic Gardens in Sydney, the vines were indeed distributed to such places as the Hunter River and Adelaide, but were then poorly propagated. It seems likely that at some stage semillon probably did grow beside riesling and became confused with it.

Shepherd's riesling was named after Thomas Shepherd who operated the Darling Nursery in Sydney in the early part of the last century. He was instrumental in providing growers with a white grape less susceptible to disease than most and one that produced good quantities of quality wine. In honour of his contribution, the grape became known as Shepherd's riesling, particularly in the Hunter Valley. It was, of course, semillon.

Fortunately for the Hunter Valley (and us), semillon is a hardy variety well suited to adverse conditions, providing good yields and, if well handled, excellent wine both dry and sweet. It very quickly became the Hunter Valley's best white wine. Its status today, even since the introduction of the more modish chardonnay, remains unchanged.

A recognised classic

In general, semillon has a stark fruity quality sometimes associated with a French chablis, and hence is commonly found in many an Australian chablis-style wine. However, given 10 years in the bottle semillon – or to be precise, Hunter Valley semillon – undergoes a complete and phenomenal transformation into a beautifully complex and beguiling wine. The breadth of flavour is quite remarkable as is the distinctive 'toastiness' (the smell of fresh toast) on the nose.

Lindemans is an acknowledged master of the style. So, too, is McWilliam's Mount Pleasant, thanks largely to the charisma of one of the early owner–winemakers, Maurice O'Shea. His ability to make great wines was acknowledged before his death in 1956, but since then has taken on legendary proportions, as tasting after tasting of 30- and 40-year-old semillons have shown.

Comparisons with the great white burgundies of France have been common (a comparison of style rather than grape variety), and in honesty it must be added that these comments were mostly made by Australians. However, in 1978 in a masked wine tasting in London organised by an American food and wine magazine, two Rothbury Estate semillons proved that the wine's Australian praise was not due entirely to parochialism. Against wines from 60 countries, including France, the two whites were ranked second and third. The winning wine was a French white burgundy.

Hunter Valley semillon is now one of the few Australian wines instantly recognisable on the European wine scene (the others being our northeastern Victorian fortified muscat and Penfold's Grange). Leading British wine writer Jancis Robinson is on record as saying: 'Great white Bordeaux and mature Hunter Valley semillon prove that the grape can provide some of the world's finest wines'.

A little sweetness perhaps

The Bordeaux mentioned above refers to semillon's birthplace in western France, an area generally better known for its red wines. The white wines of Bordeaux fall into two distinct styles. The first is a dry white table wine made with either semillon or sauvignon blanc or sometimes both, and is mainly to be found in the area called Graves. The second is an outstanding sweet dessert wine that can be found in the area called Barsac–Sauternes.

As attractive as they are, the white wines of Graves have the misfortune of living close to and under the overwhelming shadow of what is regarded as *the* greatest white wine of all – sauternes – or to be even more precise, the wines of Château d'Yquem. These wines are held up as the ideal and are the standard to which most Australian makers of dessert wines would like to aspire. To date, no Australian company has come close to the painstaking care and horrendous expense needed to make the glittering, legendary wines of d'Yquem. There is nothing to stop them trying and at least one company, run by the De Bortoli family in Griffith, New South Wales, has made a pretty determined effort.

The botrytis factor

In just 15 years Deen De Bortoli and winemaker son, Darren, have gone from making their first sauternes-style semillon to establishing the benchmark for the style in this country. It is a story of dedication and luck, in that the Griffith area should be so well suited to inducing botrytis – the vital factor in these superb, complex wines.

Botrytis is a mould that, given the right weather conditions, grows on fully ripened grapes effectively removing the grape's water and concentrating the remaining sugar and grape (and botrytis) flavours in the remaining shrivelled shell.

With De Bortoli's first botrytis semillon in 1982, the humid conditions and late vintage enabled the fruit to obtain phenomenal sugar levels producing a luscious and flavoursome wine. It was immediately greeted with rave reviews both here and overseas. Fortunately, the weather and the De Bortoli good luck continued to hold out and very fine botrytis semillon wines have been made in succeeding years.

The De Bortoli wine, now named Noble One, leads a small but impressive list of Australian botrytis semillons such as Peter Lehmann Noble Semillon, Cranswick Autumn Gold, Buller's, Wilton and Fiddler's Creek. For some reason, most winemakers interested in the style continue to use riesling and it is these wines that are far easier to find on bottleshop shelves.

Some different styles

As we have seen, semillon can take extensive bottle age to develop a rich, delicious flavour or it can have a little help – oak. Semillon's affinity with oak is matched only by that of chardonnay. After the wine has been matured in new oak casks for a couple of months and then bottled and released, it is invariably a pleasure to drink with good depth of flavour.

More and more, semillon is being blended with chardonnay to provide good quaffing wines that are also reasonably priced. This is a relatively new market niche that has been very successful, especially for those winemakers waiting for new plantings of chardonnay to come into bearing. As it can take up to three years for the first commercial crop to be harvested, immature chardonnay wine benefits from the addition of semillon.

So far we have only mentioned semillon's progress in the warmer areas of Australia, which admittedly is where much of the grape grows. Increasingly it is finding favour in cooler climates such as central and southern Victoria, Western Australia's Margaret River and Tasmania. The effect of long, cool ripening conditions has produced yet another facet to the already multitalented grape — a grassy herbaceous aroma reminiscent of sauvignon blanc. In fact, the release of the Hanging Rock Winery's semillon from Victoria's coldest wine-growing area at Macedon had wine writers in total confusion. With less sunshine to fill out the grape's flesh, the resulting wine was dry, quite acidic and had a strong herbaceous aroma. This new style of wine adds yet another different string to semillon's bow.

And now to taste
The following is a selection of Australian wines made from the semillon grape variety.

$$$

- **Brokenwood Semillon (1996)**
  A Hunter Valley style that unlike some doesn't rely on extended bottle maturation to be thoroughly enjoyable. The maker likes to promote its youthful qualities and works towards it with ripe, tangy fruit and lively acidity.
- **Hay Shed Semillon (1996)**
  The aim with this wine from the Margaret River is complexity, which is achieved through barrel fermentation and ageing. It gives a whole new perspective to semillon, adding a smoky sweetness, but most of all it provides roundness.

- **St Hallett Semillon Select (1995)**
  Barossa Valley semillon is a much under-rated variety these days, which is a shame because it often produces a wonderful alternative to chardonnay. Ripe semillon like this smells of hay, straw and citrus fruits. It tastes even better.
- **Tyrrell's Lost Block Semillon (1996)**
  Lost Block comes from the Hunter Valley and got its name because one year Murray Tyrrell forgot to order the pickers in. It was eventually picked, but late. The delicate, grapey wine relies on bottle age to make an impact. Give it five years.
- **Xanadu Semillon (1995)**
  What used to be Chateau Xanadu is now simply Xanadu but there is nothing simple about this semillon. Born in Margaret River, it shows stylish oak treatment and lashings of generous fruit.

$$

- **Cranswick Estate Semillon (1996)**
  Fermented and aged in French and American oak barrels, this Riverina wine has a distinct chardonnay feel with vanillan oak on the nose and ripe peaches on the palate. But that acidic, mouth-puckering finish is all semillon.
- **Lindemans Hunter River Bin 8655 Semillon (1995)**
  Set in the classic mould, this wine has an almost neutral

flavour now – but don't let it put you off. It will come and when it does, within the next five to 10 years, it will be a ripper. The secret is bottle maturation that will turn today's lemony clean wine into a rich, toasty masterpiece. Have patience.

- **Rosemount Estate Hunter Valley Semillon (1996)**
  Not to be confused with the show reserve semillon that is almost double the price, this modest wine has much going for it, including just a touch of sweetness to enhance the citrus flavours.

- **Tyrrell's Old Winery Semillon (1996)**
  Like the Rosemount semillon, this wine is a second stringer made to a price point. That said, it is crisp and clean with clear varietal characters such as the smell of straw, hay and lemon and a lemony flavour. Finishes dry.

- **The Willows Vineyard Semillon (1995)**
  The maker is also a winemaker at Peter Lehmann Wines, so expect some pretty nifty Barossa Valley moves, including super-ripe fruit characters, richness and superlative mouthfeel. Nothing subtle here.

$

- **Fiddlers Creek Semillon (1995)**
  Well-made, well-priced semillon from the Blue Pyrenees Estate stable with a touch of crisp, gooseberry flavour and some sweetness.

- **Krondorf Barossa Valley Semillon (1996)**
  The area may be warm but the year was cool, hence some herbaceousness on the nose, along with semillon's characteristic hay/straw. Crisp, lemon butter and citrus fruit flavours dominate.
- **Leo Buring Clare Valley Semillon (1996)**
  Firmness and flavour – that best sums up the impact this wine has in the mouth. Citrus fruit-like acid structure supports soft, floral aromas and a lemon-zesty flavour. The impression of full roundness on the middle palate comes from ripe fruit.
- **Peter Lehmann Semillon (1996)**
  This Barossa Valley maker regularly tries to make a 'dry white wine with flavour' with his semillon through partial barrel fermentation and leaving the wine in contact with its lees during oak maturation. The result is a more weighty wine in the mouth and full, citrus flavours.
- **Saltram Classic Semillon (1996)**
  This Barossa Valley semillon shows why the grape is so well suited to the region: lightly fruity in its youth, sustained by a strong acidic backbone that will also take it into the future.

Which food?

Semillon can be quite neutral and dry in flavour when young. It is a variety that blossoms with extended bottle age, producing rich honeyed flavours and a distinctive toasty aroma. As a sweet dessert style (sauternes or botrytised semillon) it is also capable of the most wonderful, luscious fruit flavours.

First course   A crisp, young semillon has an affinity with seafood: baked fish, Japanese raw fish, calamari, crayfish, baked oysters, smoked salmon.

Main course   Try an older semillon or wood-matured semillon with Indonesian and Malaysian food, roast chicken, lamb, cold smoked meats, vegetable dishes, sausages.

Dessert   A sweet style is ideal with soufflé, fruit tart or flan, light trifle, fruit cake, pavlova, fresh fruit (figs, peaches).

Cheese   Camembert, edam, gruyère, vintage cheddar.

SAUVIGNON BLANC

Sauvignon blanc is perhaps the easiest of all grape varieties to discern in a glass; it can literally knock you out with a punch of strong herbaceous smells and taste. These herbaceous characters are often present with equally strong asparagus, grassy (like the smell of newly mown grass) and gooseberry flavours. All of this makes for a fascinating if somewhat aggressive style of wine.

A relative newcomer to Australia, sauvignon blanc has become all the rage because of its crisp, dry style. Part of its popularity must be that it was one of the last great classic grape varieties to be grown here. It enjoys classic status due to its contribution in the making of some of the world's greatest dessert wines from Sauternes, as well as fine, dry, white wines from Graves in Bordeaux and the Loire Valley, in France.

Alas, in its short time here it has become reasonably clear (although there will be those who disagree) that Australia does not have the climate or the soil to make world-class sauvignon blanc – that accomplishment belongs to our neighbours across the Tasman, New Zealand. However, Australia does make some fine table wine from the grape and there has been some experimentation with dessert styles, too.

A new phenomenon

After chardonnay, the biggest white wine success story of the 1980s was sauvignon blanc or, as it is sometimes known, fumé blanc (pronounced few-may blonk). It was one of those runaway marketing success stories that swept not only the Australian wine scene but the United States, New Zealand, South Africa and even parts of South America. Sauvignon blanc was a wine very much of its time. It was fresh and tangy, made to be drunk young and highly suited to the casual bistro-style food phenomenon on whose tail it rode.

Fumé blanc is born

Sauvignon blanc is an incredibly 'obvious' grape variety: aggressive and lively in the glass. It is a brave winemaker who attempts to tame it while also maintaining its intrinsic joyous nature. Such a winemaker was Robert Mondavi, who in the United States back in 1966 attempted to tame Californian sauvignon blanc with a little oak maturation. He called it fumé blanc — a literal translation is 'smoky white'. There is an ongoing tussle among wine people worldwide whether the fumé refers to the use of oak to provide a charred, smoky character to the wine, or whether it recalls the distinctive smoky grey film that gathers on the grape in the vineyard. It probably doesn't matter which is correct. The term today represents a wine style, although it is not as common on wine shelves as it once was.

The great success of fumé blanc was due in part to marketing. The name is highly attractive, easy to pronounce and quite evocative. Mondavi's fumé blanc tamed the assertive, pungent nature of sauvignon blanc with a little ageing in oak barrels, which in turn produced a gentle, unobtrusive layer of oak in the wine. The drinker began to see some complexity (always a good thing) and more subtle flavours. Here was a wine that could be matched with a much greater variety of food than could previously be imagined.

In Australia the first winemaker to use the term 'fumé blanc' was the talented Tim Knappstein in 1978, then of Enterprise Wines in South Australia's Clare Valley (this winery is now called Tim Knappstein Wines, although Tim Knappstein himself has now moved to the Adelaide Hills). He was an early convert to the charms of the grape, being the first in the Valley to plant it. As is the way, Clare has since been overtaken in the rush to plant sauvignon blanc by almost every other wine area in the country. As is also the way, the term 'fumé blanc' appears to have had its heyday with many producers once again favouring the varietal term 'sauvignon blanc' on their labels. The generic term 'fumé blanc' could not guarantee the drinker that sauvignon blanc had been used in the making of the wine.

Conformity of style

Fumé blanc, although associated with the grape sauvignon blanc, is still a generic term and as such is open to interpretation by the winemaker. This can mean that a number of different grape varieties have been used (blends with semillon are common), with or without sauvignon blanc.

Most fumé blanc wines are dry with some wood maturation and reasonably full-bodied, but the opposite can also be true. It is not surprising then that such diverse interpretations of the style and even the grape variety have caused confusion with the consumer. For a growing number, the only way out of such a predicament is a return to the varietal name 'sauvignon blanc'. If the wine has seen some wood maturation, à la fumé blanc, you will probably see 'wood-matured sauvignon blanc' on the label. But there are always exceptions and a most notable one has been Dominique Portet at Taltarni in Victoria. He has been making a fumé blanc since 1982, and today it is not only his best-selling wine but one of the leading wines on the market. Unlike many other Australian fumé blanc and sauvignon blanc styles, which need only one year or so to show their best, the Taltarni wines can benefit from two to three years' additional ageing.

The quantity of sauvignon blanc grown in Australia is still quite small. Whether it increases or not depends largely on whether the grape can reach some kind of conformity in style rather than becoming a passing fad. Apart from the confusion over the term 'fumé blanc', there is also strong competition from New Zealand.

The New Zealand connection

Perhaps the best-known sauvignon blanc of its time on both sides of the Tasman has been the Cloudy Bay Sauvignon Blanc, which has become a standard-bearer, with its ripe, tropical fruit flavours and complexity, for the ultrasophisticated bistro set.

In the early 1980s Australian winemaker David Hohnen from Cape Mentelle in Western Australia went to New Zealand in search of a quality white wine to add to his range of reds. He came to the conclusion that New Zealand sauvignon blanc was unequalled in world-class quality and he set up a winery in the cool Marlborough region of New Zealand's South Island. The rest is history. Sales of Cloudy Bay Sauvignon Blanc jumped from 900 cases of the 1985 first release to 2900 of the 1988 and 1989 vintages. And still this is but a drop in the ocean compared with the ongoing demand for the Cloudy Bay wine.

And now to taste

The following is a selection of Australian wines made from the sauvignon blanc grape variety.

$$$

- **Alta Sauvignon Blanc (1996)**
  The King Valley's high altitude (hence, the name believe it or not) can produce clean, varietal characters and is much sought after for its grapes. Here, it stars almost entirely by itself (there is some semillon) in a breezy, non-oaked style perfect for summer.

- **Delatite Sauvignon Blanc (1996)**
  From Victoria's High Country, this maker has enjoyed considerable success over the years with her sauvignon blanc. Complexity seems to be the key with nectarines, lemons, melons and passionfruit all there in abundance along with a well-rounded finish.

- **Evans and Tate Western Australia Sauvignon Blanc (1996)**
  The key to drinking sauvignon blanc is to enjoy it in its youthful exuberance. They don't come more lively than this delightful style, with its enticing passionfruit, tropical fruit aroma and intense flavours. Finishes clean and dry.

- **Shaw and Smith Sauvignon Blanc (1995)**
  The Adelaide Hills is consistently kind to sauvignon blanc, producing not the hard, acidic and overly herbaceous styles but more easy drinking fare with soft, rounded fruity appeal and a steely structure that goes well with food.

- **Taltarni Sauvignon Blanc (1996)**
  Of the oaked and non-oaked styles made by Taltarni, this is probably the more accessible wine due in large part to its

delicious fruitiness. Smell and taste the grape with green peas and mild herbal notes mingling with a tropical tang.

$$

- **Haselgrove McLaren Vale Sauvignon Blanc (1996)**
  An up-and-coming producer with the right approach to his grapes: get them ripe and keep them clean, fresh and drinkable upon release. You couldn't want for more in a good quaffing style.
- **Lindemans Padthaway Vineyard Sauvignon Blanc (1996)**
  Padthaway is well regarded for its white wines, producing, as in this case, strong varietal characters with equally firm acidic grip. Sweet passionfruit and mildly herbal influences on the palate are highly addictive. Drink sooner rather than later.
- **Paulett's Sauvignon Blanc (1996)**
  Clare Valley's gentle warmth seems to bring the best out in this consistent performer, coaxing full, ripe flavours with a tropical fruit and gooseberry bent. It helps if the growing season is as mild as it was in 1996.
- **Preece Sauvignon Blanc (1996)**
  This new addition to Mitchelton's Preece label certainly makes its presence felt. Quite aggressive and pungent with rapier sharp acid, this sauvignon blanc is what many people still walk over broken glass for.

- **Riddoch Coonawarra Sauvignon Blanc (1996)**
  The trick in a cool year like 1996 is to achieve full ripeness. The mouthfeel and richness in this delightful expression of the sauvignon blanc grape reveals that full ripeness was indeed achieved. Herbaceousness combines with tropical fruit characters. Delicious.

$

- **Deakin Estate Sauvignon Blanc (1996)**
  You don't expect such a sophisticated taste in this price bracket, but what a delightful attack on the senses with its lovely sweet, tropical fruit aromas of passionfruit and gooseberries followed by a generous serving of flavour.
- **Deen De Bortoli Vat 2 Sauvignon Blanc (1996)**
  A simple fruity style of wine from a quality producer based in the Riverina region that sources its grapes from far and wide. Asparagus on the nose and palate gives the variety away.
- **Fiddlers Creek Sauvignon Blanc (1996)**
  Attractive in price and taste, Fiddlers Creek is the third label under Blue Pyrenees Estate. The flavours tend towards the riper spectrum with their citrussy, tropical highlights but it is the clean finish that really makes the impression here.
- **Lindemans Bin 95 Sauvignon Blanc (1996)**
  A sister release to the extremely popular Bin 65 chardonnay that, like its sibling, relies on a simple, easy-drinking,

pleasant approach. The trick, if there is one, is the sourcing of grapes from many different areas. No one regional character dominates.

- **Oxford Landing Sauvignon Blanc (1996)**
  The name comes from a Yalumba-owned vineyard in the Riverland and the wine shows the generosity of flavour and body you might expect. No surprises or highlight, just simple drinking.

Which food?

If there was ever a wine made to be served with seafood, here it is. Sauvignon blanc's powerful flavour makes it far too aggressive for many foods, but with seafood (and asparagus) it's great. Other than that, the choice of food really is rather limited compared with most grape varieties.

First course A light, crisp sauvignon blanc is highly compatible with calamari, crayfish, crab, mussels and full-flavoured fish such as snapper and John Dory, and asparagus.

Main course Choose a mature fumé blanc style (wood-matured sauvignon blanc) with mellow, creamy softness to go with pasta (with cream sauces), light curry, Chinese food.

Cheese A rich fumé blanc style goes with camembert, fetta, edam, mozzarella, vintage cheddar.

RED WINES

CABERNET SAUVIGNON

Cabernet sauvignon – sometimes called cabernet or simply cab sav – is among the most widely planted red grape varieties in the world. Its reputation as a classic grape variety producing wines of great richness and longevity is well founded, and it has the natural ability to reproduce these characteristics in most countries where it is planted. Today, that list is quite impressive: the United States, Chile, South Africa, New Zealand, France, Spain, Portugal, Italy, Greece, Bulgaria and even Lebanon.

In Australia, the grape variety is grown in large quantities right across the country and is often sold under its own name or as a blended wine. In the 1970s it was common to see it blended with shiraz (a very Australian habit that is considered unusual overseas), although nowadays winemakers tend to use other members of the cabernet sauvignon family such as cabernet franc and merlot. These wines are considered closer to the French style as practised in the home of cabernet sauvignon, Bordeaux.

The traditional wines of Bordeaux have plenty of tannin, which is important in cabernet sauvignon's ability to age well. Many Australian cabernet sauvignon wines also have this ability, although it is more common for cabernet sauvignon to be fruity and easy to drink when young. This is the way the consumer likes to enjoy cabernet sauvignon today and most wines are made to be drunk within the first five years.

The sum of many parts
Cabernet sauvignon's essential character can somehow shine through irrespective of the vineyard setting, although it is obvious that some areas are more suited than others.

As a young red wine and still quite immature it can appear leafy (herbal) and sharp on the nose, often tannic with a definite berry taste – mostly blackberry or blackcurrant. There is generally always some form of wood component in the smell and/or taste. In Australia, this can impart a spiciness, even a dusty smell. With age the combination of wood and fruit meld into even more interesting smells. Australian cabernet sauvignon has the added attraction of a eucalypt or minty smell that can be quite strong in some wines. No one knows for sure where it comes from and how it arrives in the wine.

Where it grows
Cabernet sauvignon is thought to have originated in the Middle East and was brought to France via the Roman legions. Its home there is the Medoc in Bordeaux where the climate is quite cool and the soil well drained and gravelly.

In Australia, the sites that have revealed the closest connection with those of France are equally cool and with characteristic soils – South Australia's Coonawarra and Adelaide Hills, Victoria's Yarra Valley, Bendigo and Mornington Peninsula and Western Australia's Margaret River.

Coonawarra, in southern South Australia, close to the Victorian border, is generally acknowledged as producing some of our finest cabernet sauvignon wines. The secret is said to lie in the soil, more specifically, a strip of red earth called terra rossa that runs in a line 15 kilometres long and varies in width from just 200 metres to 1.5 kilometres.

Wine companies pay high prices for such land and not surprisingly most of the terra rossa is planted with vines. There is a lot of myth surrounding its wonderous properties; suffice to say, limestone found only underneath the red strip is an important key and helps with drainage. Vines do not like wet feet.

In cooler areas like Coonawarra a long, cool ripening period for the grape concentrates a richness of flavour in cabernet sauvignon that can be quite aggressive and tannic. Time in the bottle helps to make it more palatable. The alternative is to blend cabernet sauvignon with another grape variety to make a softer, more appealing young wine.

In warmer areas like South Australia's Barossa Valley, the Hunter Valley in New South Wales and northeastern Victoria, cabernet sauvignon ripens so well that there is less need to blend, the fruit having become quite fat with warm, sweet flavours. Higher alcohol can be easily obtained with a resulting increase in the body of the wine. 'Big', 'gutsy' and even 'macho' are common adjectives used to describe these wines in which northeastern Victoria in particular specialises. Preserved as it were by high alcohol and a mass of powerful fruit, these wines are quite capable of appearing fresh and lively at 10 or 20 years of age.

In the past, these big mouth-filling wines were labelled the quintessential Australian reds overseas. Today, the trend is towards wines made for earlier consumption with a little more finesse.

How it is made

By itself cabernet sauvignon is capable of making some very fine wines but it can also be rather simple, what winemakers like to call 'one-dimensional'. As full of flavour as it can be, sometimes it isn't enough. Sometimes what is needed is a touch of spice, a little more complexity, finesse! That's when winemakers reach for a blending partner.

In Australia the first great blending grape to suit cabernet sauvignon's personality was shiraz. From a European viewpoint it is a very strange bedfellow indeed, since in France the two are grown in separate regions and are divided by tradition as well as law. In Australia no such traditions exist and so as shiraz was plentiful it was a logical move. While some great wines were made, the style was misunderstood overseas, especially in important export markets like England and the United States. Today, you will find an increasing number of cabernet sauvignon wines blended with a little merlot, cabernet franc and malbec. This is in keeping with acknowledged French tradition as practised in Bordeaux and as such is far more familiar to the European and American palates. The move is also said to have brought elegance to Australian cabernet sauvignon.

Besides the quality of the fruit, the other great contribution to cabernet sauvignon's taste and elegance is the wood cask that is used to mature the newly made wine. In the past, large oak barrels were the popular choice, partly due to cost and partly due to tradition. However, being used every vintage for years and years may have been economical but it often left the barrels stale, a taste that was, sadly, imparted to the wine.

The late Max Schubert, a winemaker at Penfolds, first began using small oak barrels for his famous Grange Hermitage wines (now simply called Grange) during the 1950s. Small barrels of new wood were used, no larger than 300 litres in capacity, to bring the wine into an increased area of contact with wood and hence greater extraction of tannin from the wood. The best French wines employed the practice and gradually Australian winemakers, too, converted to small, new oak casks. This was despite the additional costs involved in the importation of the oak and the limited use of the wood for just a couple of vintages.

Cabernet sauvignon is most suited to French oak's mellow smokiness, while American oak with its strong vanilla characters is generally considered too aggressive for the grape.

There is no doubt that the use of new oak maturation has contributed not only a freshness and vitality to cabernet sauvignon but improved its ability to age more gracefully.

And now to taste

The following is a selection of Australian wines made from the cabernet sauvignon grape variety.

$$$

- **Evans and Tate Margaret River Cabernet Sauvignon (1994)**

  Twenty-four months' maturation in oak indicates a serious wine – the winemaker is obviously confident the wine can take such extended time in the barrel. The result is a lean, tight and noticeably tannic wine. Relies on further bottle maturation to reward the drinker.

- **Mitchelton Victoria Cabernet Sauvignon (1994)**

  Different regions have each made a contribution to this exciting wine. Very drinkable now with ripe, blackberry aromas on the nose. The medium-bodied palate has intense blackcurrant flavours. Supple, with lifted finish.

- **Oakridge Estate Reserve Cabernet Sauvignon (1994)**

  No expense has been spared by this classy Yarra Valley winery. The best fruit and the best oak have resulted in a stylish wine brimming with soft, vanillan oak characters and delicious ripe and spicy blackberry flavours.

- **Tollana Bin TR 222 Cabernet Sauvignon (1994)**

  The Eden Valley is rarely thought of as a red wine area but this example will make you think twice. Generous blackberry characters, smoky aromas and tobacco on the nose, and rounded cassis on the palate make this wine enjoyable now, but it will be even more so within six years.

- **Wirra Wirra Vineyards The Angelus (1994)**
  McLaren Vale and Coonawarra cabernet sauvignon mingle together in the bottle here, the former providing good blackberry aromas and a strong mainframe, the latter filling out the hollows with more subtle nuances.

$$

- **Preece Cabernet Sauvignon (1994)**
  Named in honour of legendary Victorian wine man Colin Preece, this wine made by Mitchelton is a great legacy with its skillful blending of different cabernet sauvignon parcels to make a highly drinkable, berry and cherry-flavoured wine with subtle oak handling.

- **Renmano Chairman's Selection Cabernet Sauvignon (1994)**
  Always a source of generous, ripe fruit and equally measured oak, this Riverland favourite from the BRL Hardy empire offers amazing value for money. This particular vintage, with its higher acidity, is slightly different from the norm.

- **Sandalford Caversham Cabernet Sauvignon Shiraz (1994)**
  This is a reminder of the successful and typically Aussie

blend of cabernet and shiraz that used to be so prevalent. Shiraz brings a real sweetness to the wine, while cabernet gives it weight.

- **Seppelt Terrain Series Cabernet Sauvignon (1994)**
  A new label at an economical price showing off a strong minty aroma (central Victorian dare we suggest?) with lots of rich, berry fruit and tannic support. Can age an additional five years.

- **Woodstock Cabernet Sauvignon (1994)**
  Historically McLaren Vale is better known for its shiraz, but those who seek out big-bodied cabernets like this one are rarely disappointed. The level of sweet oak on the nose and cinnamon and spicy fruit on the palate reveal a wine that has yet to fully integrate. Give it another five years.

$

- **Deakin Estate Cabernet Sauvignon (1995)**
  From the Murray Valley, this producer (formerly Sunnycliff) has built a reputation on good-flavoured wines like this one, with its earthy aroma and sweet oak and dusty flavours.

- **Deen De Bortoli Vat 9 Cabernet Sauvignon (1995)**
  This De Bortoli label, named in honour of the Riverina pioneering winemaker and founder, Deen De Bortoli, is a consistent performer in tastings. The reason is simple.

The quality of this delightfully full-flavoured wine defies the price asked.

- **Hardy's Nottage Hill Cabernet Shiraz (1994)**
  Another reminder of a blended style that used to be all the rage, and that has never really gone out of fashion. With its generous, softy fruity appeal, why should it?

- **McWilliams Hanwood Cabernet Sauvignon (1994)**
  A Riverina-made cabernet that relies on a softly, softly approach with developed flavours and earthy appeal rather than mind-blowing oak and concentrated fruitiness. Pretty tame but enjoyable.

- **Rosemount Estate Cabernet Sauvignon (1995)**
  Hunter Valley cabernet sauvignon in all its youthfulness: smell and taste the sweet, macerated cherries. So delightfully simple and fruity.

Which food?

Cabernet sauvignon can make a blockbuster of a red wine – a big mouthful of a wine displaying an astonishing depth of flavour and richness – and therefore needs the benefit of similarly rich food in order to be digested and enjoyed. At the other extreme is the light and fruity rosé, and in between, the medium-bodied, pleasant-tasting wine that can also be quite elegant. Because of the many different styles it is always best to try to match the 'weight' of the wine with the 'weight' of the food being presented; that is, hearty stews with a robust cabernet sauvignon, light pasta dishes with rosé.

Pre-dinner drinks   Cabernet rosé.

Hors d'oeuvre   Paté, dip, terrine, meat savouries.

First course   Gnocchi, mussels (light reds), warm spinach, bacon and mushroom salad.

Main course   Roast beef or lamb, coq au vin, grilled steak, casserole, rabbit, sausages, hamburgers, meat pies.

Cheese   Vintage cheddar, stilton, brie, blue-vein, gouda, parmesan.

After-dinner drinks   Cabernet port.

SHIRAZ

If cabernet sauvignon is the aristocrat of the red wine world, the often neglected workhorse is shiraz. As the basis of so many of our fortified and table wines and even sparklings, shiraz has been the backbone of Australia's red wine production for decades.

When substantial plantings of cabernet sauvignon in the last century were wiped out by the vine insect phylloxera, it was shiraz that took their place.

In the 1950s when winemaker (the late) Max Schubert at Penfolds wanted to make a red wine to rival those of Bordeaux, he had to turn to shiraz because he could find virtually no cabernet sauvignon in Australia. Fortunately for all wine lovers shiraz was up to the job and a unique Australian wine – Grange – was born.

Growing on the grape's reputation for fine wines were the shiraz wines of Coonawarra, South Australia, and the Hunter Valley, New South Wales. To many, shiraz's home in Australia is the Hunter Valley and older patrons of the style will fondly recall the wine's peculiar and distinctive Hunter aroma known as 'sweaty saddle'. Although this is still seen (or rather, smelt) from time to time, better winemaking techniques are gradually resulting in much cleaner and, to some, more acceptable aromas.

Shiraz's versatility in the winery and its adaptability in the vineyard endear it to many a winemaker and drinker alike. Shiraz seems to encapsulate the essence of Australia with its open, uncomplicated flavours and earthy appeal.

An indigenous style

Australians love shiraz. We have the largest plantings of the grape in the world, around 6000 hectares or three times the land area devoted to the grape in its true home in France's Rhône Valley.

Shiraz represents about one-tenth of all grapes crushed in Australia each year and it is not surprising to learn that it is grown in almost every wine-growing district across the continent. Only Tasmania, our coldest State, is without significant plantings.

The key to high yields of shiraz fruit is warmth, and in

the hot regions around the Murray River it is not uncommon for yields to reach an astonishing 20 tonnes to the hectare. On that point alone, it is easy to see why shiraz is much loved. Such economy makes it an essential ingredient in many of our lower-priced cask wines, generic-labelled reds and fortified wines that flow from the Riverland in South Australia and the Riverina in New South Wales. These are the bread-and-butter wines of the Australian wine industry. They are well-made everyday drinking styles notable for their generous fruit and characteristic spiciness, which is one of shiraz's trademarks. Its other – a pronounced peppery taste – is more likely to arise in shiraz grown in slightly cooler locations. Here, yield is deliberately kept low (through non-irrigation and pruning) to concentrate flavour in the grapes.

Cool-climate shiraz can be very different from its warm-area cousin, producing at times quite intense spicy and peppery characters together with a sharp raspberry–blackcurrant taste. With the use of different oak barrels for maturation, for example, American and French oak, shiraz from a cool area can take on a whole new dimension. It is these wines that so often favourably compare with the highest quality cabernet sauvignon. It is unfortunate that for a while many of us never sought to taste them. In the rush for the new and the trendy, like cabernet sauvignon and pinot noir, these wines were often overlooked.

Luckily, the cyclic nature of trends, where the old is new again, has seen a rise once more in shiraz's fortunes. It could be said that only a truly classic grape variety could stage such a comeback.

Overseas, shiraz continues to be seen as a peculiarly indigenous wine style almost unique to Australia. This has been both a plus and a minus. The United States has only small plantings of the grape and as such consumers are not used to the wine, but this is slowly changing. Companies like Rosemount Estate are doing well exporting rich, oaked styles, while a group of American winemakers, who call themselves cheekily 'The Rhône Rangers', are introducing shiraz to a wider audience, which will no doubt be capitalised upon by the Australian industry. However, there is a little problem over the name or rather a problem of too many names.

Hermitage? Syrah? Shiraz?

Historians are confident that the existence of a town called Shiraz in southeastern modern-day Iran is where it all started. Excavations have put forward the reasonable assumption that the grape came to France via the Mediterranean and was nicely settled in its new home in the Rhône Valley by the time of the Roman Empire.

The French call shiraz 'syrah' (pronounced cee-rah) and in the northern Rhône it finds its finest expression in the wines of Hermitage among others. This last name should be most familiar to many an Australian wine drinker, for it is the name some winemakers have used when they mean shiraz. It has also been the favoured name of some Hunter Valley vignerons.

Shiraz and hermitage are one and the same thing in this

country, although there is some pressure for the grape to be uniformly labelled as shiraz, since using the term 'hermitage' refers to an existing French product. Australian winemakers are certainly not allowed to export to Europe wines featuring that name as it is forbidden by European Union regulations.

Shiraz has had its fair share of name-calling. A well-publicised conversion from shiraz to the name 'French syrah' was made some years ago by Taltarni winemaker Dominique Portet, who is French-born. He insists the name change resulted in extra sales, such was the low esteem the name 'shiraz' was held in at the time. However, only a few years later, solicitors acting for the French wine industry contacted Mr Portet and persuaded him that since his grapes were not French-born as well, he could not use the name. He has since reverted to using the term shiraz.

But back to the northern Rhône, where the syrah grape can produce wines so rich and tannic that it is sometimes necessary to add a small percentage of white grapes (up to 20 per cent) in order for the finished product to appear better balanced. This does not happen in Australia. Although we, too, have a tradition of big, healthy, tannic shiraz wines, especially from northeastern Victoria and the Hunter Valley in New South Wales, drinkers down through the generations have come to recognise and enjoy the style. Those who haven't have sought out a blending of shiraz with cabernet sauvignon. Another notable difference between the syrah of France and the shiraz of Australia is the often strong and all-pervading fragrance and taste of mint in our wines. This is sometimes thought to become pronounced by the use of small new oak casks to mature the wine in, the current Australian obsession.

The French do not use new oak each year. A mixture of larger-sized oak casks made from old as well as new oak is believed to provide a better-balanced wine. In our enthusiasm and in the belief that shiraz can gain added complexity as cabernet sauvignon does through new oak maturation, there has been huge investment in oak. This seems to date back to the birth of Penfolds Grange and while not everyone wants to make that style today, there is little doubt that this nearly 50-year-old wine style is the apex to which many Australian winemakers aspire.

Grange

Grange is a wine that was created amid much controversy in the 1950s by the Penfolds wine company in South Australia. Today it is widely regarded as Australia's most recognised wine overseas, regularly receiving the plaudits of wine writers, and on its home turf it is probably our single greatest wine. A bottle of 1951 Grange was sold in 1998 for $24 000, an Australian record.

The man who first made Grange, Max Schubert (who died in 1994), introduced many new and controversial winemaking techniques that today are largely taken for granted, and he set the scene for a re-evaluation of shiraz as a most notable wine rather than a workhorse.

Following a visit to Bordeaux in France, a young Max

Schubert became interested in making a wine that would last 20 years and a wine of quality that 'would bring it recognition in France, but [it would be] an Australian wine with an individual Australian character'. The year was 1951.

Max Schubert's original choice was cabernet sauvignon but as there was precious little of the grape around he settled on shiraz. Importantly, he chose shiraz from cooler areas, not from the hot (and at that time) port-producing regions. He crushed the grapes, cooled the resulting must (unfermented grape juice), pumped the wine into open concrete fermentation tanks and then with specially constructed 'heading down' boards he forcefully kept the juice and the skins, pips and stalks (solids) completely immersed during fermentation. This allowed for the full extraction of colour and tannins from the grapes, essential for long-living wines. Fermentation lasted an amazing 12 days rather than the usual three. Also completely new to Australia was the use of five new American oak hogsheads (300-litre capacity) into which the wine was put and stored at a cool temperature.

Within one month he began to notice quite remarkable changes. 'The volume of bouquet comprising raw oak mixed with natural varietal fruit was tremendous', said Schubert during an interview in 1988 when he was named *Decanter* wine magazine's Man of the Year. 'The overall flavour was much more intense and for a big, young wine the balance was superb.' After 18 months' oak maturation the wine was bottled and cellared before release. Today, it is released with at least six years' bottle age.

Although not immediately liked by wine writers and Schubert's peers, the wine has since become the stuff of legends, the 1955 Grange picking up 170 major awards at Australian wine shows, making it probably the most decorated wine in Australian history.

Grange was also the impetus for other successful shiraz-based wines from the Penfolds stable – St Henri, Bin 128, Kalimna. It also proved important inspiration to modern-day master red winemaker, Wolf Blass.

And now to taste

The following is a selection of Australian wines made from the shiraz grape variety.

$$$

- **Blackjack Shiraz (1994)**
  A new central Victorian winery producing extraordinary shiraz wines that brim to overflow with fruit and integrated, classy oak. The oak gives a smooth, fine texture, while the sweet, spicy berry and cinnamon flavours provide the real focus.
- **Bleasdale Sparkling Shiraz (non vintage)**
  A truly indigenous sparkling style that can take some time to warm to, warm being the operative word. Sourced from Langhorne Creek, this warm wine is rich in sweet fruit with a spicy flavour. More-ish in the extreme.

- **David Wynn Unwooded Shiraz (1996)**
  The late David Wynn is said to have been amused by the number of over-oaked wines around. His winemaker son, Adam, believes he has found the answer. The colour is just extraordinary: a vibrant garnet–purple. Summer pudding fruits dominate: raspberries, cherries, strawberries. Will age.
- **Norman's Old Vine Shiraz (1995)**
  Cassis, cassis and more cassis – this new release from the South Australian Norman's stable capitalises on the rich, concentrated grape flavours achieved from low-yielding aged vines. It is an incredibly generous, full-on shiraz that will only get better and better. Give it another six to eight years.
- **Seaview Edwards and Chaffey McLaren Vale Shiraz (1994)**
  One of the real stars of 1996 that enchanted many with its fruit and oak complexity (the latter from 12 months in French oak) and length of flavour in the mouth. A new top-of-the-range red for Seaview that delivers drinkability now but has huge potential for ageing.

$$

- **Lakewood Shiraz (1996)**
  Released as a mere babe in nappies, don't expect to age this wine for any length of time. Enjoy as soon as possible for its simple, fruity charm and gentle toastiness.

- **Montrose Black Shiraz (1994)**
  Launched in 1996, this shiraz from Mudgee-based producer Montrose (part of Orlando Wyndham) was an instant hit, given the great combination of rich, ripe fruit and loads of toasty American oak.

- **Plunkett's Blackwood Ridge Shiraz (1995)**
  Drinkers either love or hate the minty, eucalypt characters inherent in many central Victorian reds. The smell and taste is particularly noticeable and delightful in this wine, which is both full bodied and full flavoured with a peppery, blackberry intensity.

- **Riddoch Coonawarra Shiraz (1994)**
  Smell the earth! But the earthiness soon gives way to more berry and oak-derived flavours. The fact that you can still see them as separate entities indicates the wine's youth. Needs time to fully integrate.

- **Trentham Estate Shiraz (1994)**
  A real surprise to many shiraz lovers, this rich, earthy shiraz hails from across the Murray River in New South Wales. The surprise comes in the concentrated, blackberry fruit you might expect to see from cooler areas. Another surprise is its ageing ability.

$

- **Angove's Classic Reserve Shiraz (1994)**
  'Classic Reserve' certainly sounds impressive, but the

price and wine quality are a little more egalitarian. South Australia's Riverland delivers the goods once more with lots of fruit, body, flavour and a smidgeon of tannin for short-term ageing.

- **Banrock Station Shiraz (1994)**
  Produced under the BRL Hardy umbrella, this new line made from Riverland fruit shows the kind of dried, leathery smells and baked flavours we have come to associate with hot regions. Big and simple. Do not age.

- **Deen De Bortoli Vat 8 Shiraz (1995)**
  A Riverina wine that shows shiraz in all its plummy, earthy richness on the nose and spicy, blackberry sweetness on the palate. Has length and even the ability to age well (try up to five years).

- **Renmano Chairman's Selection Bin 304 Hermitage (1994)**
  Like its cabernet sauvignon equivalent, this hermitage (shiraz, that is) is jam-packed with ripe fruit. Somewhat unusual at this price point, it also shows sweet, toasty oak.

- **Rosemount Shiraz (1995)**
  Youthful it certainly is, with simple, fruity, cherry, berry flavours. Its release one year after vintage indicates that it is intended for early consumption. Do not age.

Which food?

Shiraz, in its many forms, has an ability to match many different foods, from the sparkling shiraz style now enjoying a come-back to the easy-quaffing and rich, spicy examples so popular right now. What was said about cabernet sauvignon applies equally to shiraz: match the 'weight' of the wine to the 'weight' of the food.

Pre-dinner drinks   Sparkling shiraz.

Hors d'oeuvre   Cheese in filo pastry, pâté, meat savouries.

First course   Mussels, pasta, stuffed mushrooms, devilled kidneys, quail salad (lighter style).

Main course   Roast lamb or beef, grilled steak, coq au vin and chicken dishes with sauces, roast veal, venison, pasta, duck, goose, meat pies, sausages, hamburgers, and turkey and pork (sparkling shiraz).

Cheese   Brie, mild or mature cheddar, parmesan, gouda, gorgonzola.

PINOT NOIR

The pinot noir grape, responsible for some of the great wines of France, is the Australian wine industry's latest challenge. As with any new grape variety it is a matter of finding the most suitable soil and climate as well as winemaking techniques. Enthusiastic and dedicated Australian winemakers have already started producing some fine red table wines.

Pinot noir's other important role is inside the bottles of French champagne and other sparkling wines. This may seem a strange place for a red wine grape when most champagne is creamy white in colour, but this is also part of the allure of pinot noir. The flavour and structure the grape gives to a sparkling wine are obviously worth the incredible trouble the winemaker must go to to keep the grapes unbroken before pressing. This is to avoid the pigmentation from the skins of the black grapes colouring the juice. For the same reason, the grapes are pressed as quickly as possible.

In Australia, plantings of the grape have always been small, and pinot noir didn't really find its niche until the 1970s when, on the advice of a friend, winemaker Murray Tyrrell in the Hunter Valley, New South Wales, set out to develop a lighter, finer style of red wine and chose pinot noir. In 1979 his 1976 pinot noir made world headlines when it won first place above some of the greatest French wines at the Paris Wine Olympiad. It was later to feature in *Time* magazine as one of the 10 greatest wines in the world. Naturally, interest in the wine at home was heightened. Little was known of it at the time and plantings were small, but not for long.

Pinot noir was coveted as a wine style that would do well. In stark contrast to the heavy Australian red wine of the day, pinot noir was noticeably lighter in body, with strawberry and floral overtones, a tinge of sweetness and a velvety soft flavour. However, most winemakers were completely unprepared for the grape's contrary nature. It is a low yielder and is susceptible to spring frosts and all manner of diseases.

Worse, there are reportedly more than 1000 different types or clones of pinot noir and it soon became apparent that Australian winemakers were in receipt of more than their fair share of poor clonal material.

Many wines lacked colour, richness, body and tannin. They had little resemblance to some of the better wines of Burgundy in France with their velvety softness and elegance.

It soon became obvious that unravelling the mysteries of pinot noir would take some time. This is certainly the prevailing mood today.

Unravelling the mysteries

Some winemakers seem quite happy to trade in on pinot noir's current popularity, charging high prices for some ordinary wines. Others are more anxious to continue the hunt for quality. Some obvious signposts marking the way relate to climate, soil and traditional French winemaking techniques. Many winemakers are looking to Burgundy, pinot noir's home, for clues.

Pinot noir finds its greatest expression in the fabled vineyards of Burgundy's Côte de Nuits. The Burgundians, while basking in the admiration that pinot noir has brought them, are also aware of the criticism that comes from growing this most perplexing of grape varieties. It is often said that Burgundy produces some of the best and worst wines in the world. These are valuable lessons to be learnt from the Australian winemakers' viewpoint.

With some notable exceptions, Burgundy often lacks

sufficient sunshine to achieve full ripeness and depth of flavour in the grapes. The Burgundian response is to add sugar to achieve a higher alcohol content and improve the wine's balance. But sometimes they add too much and rob the wine of its character. Australian winemakers, too, are seeking out the cooler climates for pinot noir, most notably in Tasmania, the Adelaide Hills in South Australia, Margaret River in Western Australia, and southern Victoria around the Mornington Peninsula, Yarra Valley and Geelong regions. But as in Burgundy, the sun does not always shine and Australian winemakers do not have the benefit of being allowed to add sugar. This has helped to make the growing of pinot noir very much a hit-and-miss affair, and there have been calls for our winemakers to be allowed to add sugar.

As in Burgundy, having created a market for pinot noir is one thing but satisfying it is another. With the new cooler climate vineyards still in their infancy and very shy-yielding, the logical move has been to plant pinot noir in warmer areas. Here, the sun does its work perhaps too well, and the result has often been pinot noir that is heavy and alcoholic with little finesse.

The other extreme has been a proliferation of what are termed 'strawberry cordials', wines that have the characteristic strawberry nose but are thin and lifeless.

Two tastes

Pinot noir's popularity means you will see a whole range of differing styles available as winemakers everywhere have a go at growing it. No single style has come to capture the drinker's imagination, but like chardonnay and cabernet sauvignon before it, Australians are increasingly becoming polarised to one of two main tastes.

The first is a noticeably lighter and finer wine in both colour and body with a gentle delicacy of strawberry or cherry flavour or both, but not too delicate. Acidity and tannin are there in reserve for later on as the wine concentrates flavour with age.

Two successful exponents of this style have been wine writer and maker James Halliday with his Coldstream Hills pinot noir from the Yarra Valley and Mornington Peninsula's Stonier's Winery pinot noir. Both wine styles regularly do well in magazine wine tastings.

The second major style of pinot noir is relatively heavy and rich in fruit flavour and alcohol. King of this category is the voluptuous Bannockburn pinot noir from Geelong. Winemaker Gary Farr is a regular participant at vintage in Burgundy and since the mid-1980s has moved towards classic Burgundian winemaking methods. He is also a firm believer in the importance of the right soil and favours a limestone base, like the composition of much of Burgundy, for drainage and root penetration. Pinot noir, like all grape varieties, does not like getting its feet wet. During dry periods limestone can also provide reserves of water, which is most useful.

Winemaking

After decades of perfecting winemaking technology to make the cleanest possible wines, many winemakers are realising they may be removing too much of the wine's character. This is true of pinot noir.

Processes like racking the wine – drawing the wine off the solids that collect at the bottom of the barrel or tank – can cause the wine to dry up and lose fruit flavour if performed too often. Winemakers are becoming careful to keep pinot noir's delicate (some would say, fragile) nature intact. After working to maximise colour, aroma and tannin it would be foolish to remove these important qualities through the often brutal punishment involved in numerous rackings and filtration (the clarifying of the wine before bottling).

Other Burgundian techniques finding favour include the fermentation of whole, uncrushed berries (to extract colour, aroma and tannin from the skins) as well as the inclusion of grape stalks for increased tannin, which helps with the wine's longevity. Fermentation is often completed in new oak barrels where contact with the lees (deposit of dead yeast cells and other solids) produces a softness and a velvety wine texture.

And now to taste
The following is a selection of Australian wines made from the pinot noir grape variety.

$$$

- **Dalrymple Vineyards Pinot Noir (1995)**
  This small Tasmanian producer from the Pipers Brook

area in the north of the State has gone in for a big, voluptuous style of pinot. Sweaty and earthy on the nose, it fills out on the palate with sweet raspberry and blackberry jam flavours. Note the smooth oak component.

- **Devil's Lair Pinot Noir (1995)**
  From the Margaret River region, this young pinot has a rustic, raw quality to it. Leathery and gamy aromas flow on to a medium-bodied palate developing some intriguing forest, fungal flavours.

- **Lillydale Vineyards Pinot Noir (1995)**
  This young Yarra Valley pinot noir is still coming to grips with its multi-faceted self. Time should bring those delicious beetroot and earthy aromas into line with the full, sweet, earthy flavours and grainy oak tannins on the palate.

- **Stonier's Winery Pinot Noir (1995)**
  A consistent performer in shows and tastings, this delightful pinot noir from the Mornington Peninsula is what good pinot noir is all about: sweet, stewed cherries on the nose with loads of plums combined with discreet oak handling on the palate.

- **Pipers Brook Vineyard Pellion Pinot Noir (1995)**
  One of the stars on the Australian pinot noir scene, hailing from Tasmania, with the accent on super-clean fruitiness with underlying tannic strength. Taste the strawberries, cherries and sweet vanillan oak straight up, then that full middle palate spicy complexity comes into play. Simply delicious.

$$

Because of the high cost of production, it is hard to find pinot noir at this price point.

- **Windy Peak Victoria Pinot Noir (1996)**
  A quality pinot noir made at De Bortoli Yarra Valley with grapes sourced from around Victoria. This multi-district sourcing has yielded great results: lively cherry berry aromas, delightfully fruity palate with fine-grain tannins for support.

- **Queen Adelaide Pinot Noir (1996)**
  Wine drinkers should not expect a strong pinot noir varietal character here. The accent appears to be quite firmly on sweetish confectionery characters.

- **Rowan Pinot Noir (1995)**
  A second label under the St Hubert's brand, Rowan attempts to provide good wine at smart prices. This pinot noir succeeds in drinkability with a fine pinot tannic grip.

- **Tyrrell's Old Winery Pinot Noir (1995)**
  This Hunter Valley pinot relies on plenty of fruit and upfront freshness for its appeal. The colour is light cherry, which can also be tasted on the palate, along with strawberries. Drink while fresh and lively.

- **David Wynn Pinot Noir (1995)**
  Soft and supple, the emphasis of this wine, made by Mountadam in the Adelaide Hills, is on simple fruity appeal with some typical pinot noir hallmarks evident, such as cherry flavours and gentle tannins. Enjoy early on.

$

Because of the high cost of production, it is all but impossible to find pinot noir at this price point.

Which food?
A good pinot noir is a joy to behold and taste in conjunction with equally good food. The best styles are usually quite subtle with a hint of sweetness, and care should be taken not to overwhelm them.

Pre-dinner drinks   A pinot noir sparkling wine (méthode champenoise).

First course   Pasta with meat sauce, fish (especially Atlantic salmon), chicken, cold meats.

Main course   Roast pork, nouvelle cuisine lamb dishes, duck, squab, pheasant.

Cheese   Brie, camembert, leicester.

FORTIFIED WINES

Fortified wines are those wine styles that many of us like to finish a meal with – port, muscat, tokay and brandy. The exception is sherry, which is generally served before the meal starts and is called an apéritif from the French word meaning appetiser. As an apéritif it is designed to stimulate the palate for the meal ahead, and at the end of a meal a fortified wine can also aid the digestive process (digestif).

These wines, usually quite heavy in alcohol as the name suggests, are not meant to be drunk in huge quantities or very quickly. They are served in small glasses and are sipped in order to be savoured.

FORTIFYING THE SPIRIT!

The problem, if that is the right word, is that fortified wines are just as their name suggests, strong in taste and alcohol. Alcohol content (between 17 and 20 per cent by volume) is often double that of most table wines and hence the reticence on behalf of some to imbibe.

The fact that many fortifieds like port, tokay and muscat have traditionally been served at the end of the meal has also had a marked influence. Licensed restaurants have recorded a marked downturn in fortified wine sales since the introduction of harsh drink–driving penalties and breathalysers.

No such fears of going 'over the top' apply to the equally alarming decline in sherry sales, for it is generally served as an apéritif. Here, fashion seems to have played a large role in deciding its gloomy future. Viewed unkindly as a 'lady's drink', it has forever been associated with weddings, Christmas, or, worse, park benches. The truth is, fortified wines and their myriad tastes, from the driest to the sweetest, can develop a rich beauty and complexity that no interested wine drinker can afford to ignore.

One part of the secret is in the processes employed. The basic 'recipe' calls for the addition of extra alcohol, either grape spirit or brandy, during or after the partial or complete fermentation of the wine. The other part lies with the winemaker and the art of blending various parcels of completed wines from various vintage years into magical offerings.

Australia does make some of the best fortified wines in the world and despite the obvious cost involved in making, storing and ageing, they are among our best bargains. Be aware when buying any of our fortifieds in the future that the Australian wine industry's trade agreement with Europe will see the gradual phasing out of familiar names like port, sherry and tokay. In fact, producers are already looking at alternative descriptions now.

PORT

A number of port styles exist of which tawny and vintage are the most common.

Tawny port

Tawny port is normally a blend of wines from different years, matured in oak casks and fortified with high-strength fortifying spirit. This extended oak maturation results in a generally lighter colour (hence the name), aroma and flavour.

The gentle oxidation process (air coming through the cask into the wine) breaks down the red colour of the wine into shades of amber brown with time, which can be anything from six to 12 years – 30 years and more is not unheard of. Old wood is favoured, for it allows the gradual imparting of concentrated wood flavour (new wood would produce too sharp a flavour).

Tawny is by far the most popular port style today, largely due to its very pleasant drink-now qualities. When it is released it is considered at its optimum and unlikely to improve further.

Favoured grape varieties are cabernet sauvignon, mataro, shiraz and grenache.

Because it is a blend of different vintages, tawny port does not carry a vintage year on the label. Unlike vintage port, a tawny can be safely left open for long periods of time without risk of spoilage.

Vintage port

Vintage port carries a date on the label because it is made of wine from a single year. Unlike tawny port, it is matured for only a short time in oak casks, one to two years, and is generally not ready for drinking upon release.

Vintage port needs extended bottle age, which is usually left to the buyer to do, before it is ready to reveal its secrets, and a general rule of thumb is 10 years from the date of vintage (less if it is a half-bottle because the wine matures faster). It is usually fortified with brandy spirit containing about 80 per cent alcohol and is heavier in body, darker in colour and all round more substantial than the majority of tawny ports.

Australian winemakers are starting to try Portuguese grape varieties like touriga and bastardo for their vintage ports, which is adding interest to a wine style definitely not considered fashionable. A contributing factor to its unfashionability is that after ageing the wine for 10 years or more it should be drunk on the day or night it is opened. It does not keep well once opened.

White port

White port simply indicates that the port has been made from white wine grapes. The colour is still brown, although perhaps a little lighter than many ports, because of wood contact and the role of oxidation. Not a very common style.

Ruby port

Ruby port is another style of port that is no longer as fashionable as it once was. Ruby by name and ruby by colour, this port spends less time in oak casks than tawny port, thereby keeping its ruby red colour. Light and fruity, it is made to drink quite early on, which has caused its detractors to note it is not a serious port style.

Late bottle vintage port (LBV)

LBV, as it is known, is a vintage port that has been left in oak casks for an extended period in order to develop further complexity.

There is much interest in this style overseas and a few examples exist in Australia.

SHERRY

It is often suggested that Australian sherries can equal, if not better, the finest in Spain, the birthplace of sherry. Yet for many years winemakers had little success producing sherries bearing anything but the slightest resemblance to those from Spain.

Few improvements were made until the 1930s when researchers at Roseworthy Agricultural College in South Australia started to investigate the mysteries of sherry production in Spain. They concentrated on the flor or yeast that grows on the surface of some of the finest Spanish sherries, imparting a distinctive nutty flavour that is unique.

Flor

Selection of a suitable light and delicate base wine for flor sherry is of great importance, not only to support the yeast but to acquire its flavour and aroma. Palomino and pedro ximinez are the two most suitable sherry grapes, but only the latter is available in any great quantities in Australia and is used for oloroso styles. Suitable substitutes have been sultana, doradillo and muscat.

Flor yeast holds the key to many of the better styles of sherry that are made in Australia today — fino, amontillado, manzanilla and oloroso.

Fino
Matured under the flor yeast, fino is generally very dry, delicate and slightly nutty. Rewards early drinking. It can take time to acquire the taste for fino, considered the connoisseur's wine.

Amontillado
More generous to taste than fino and favoured for its warm nuttiness from wood maturation and medium dryness, amontillado is matured under flor yeast early in life and then aged further (in wood), becoming darker in colour, increasing in alcoholic strength and losing the freshness usually associated with finos. Amontillado is a favourite wine to serve with soups.

Manzanilla
Very few Australian winemakers persist with this light dry fino-type sherry. It is a specialist wine from Spain.

Oloroso
Oloroso is matured without the flor yeast. Slow oxidation (contact with the air) is its secret, creating a full-bodied sweeter style that is quite dark in colour and rich in taste. Cream and commercial 'sweet' sherries are of this style.

Solera blending

Second in importance behind the use of flor in the production of fine sherry is the complicated solera blending system of maturation in which casks of wine on flor yeast are stacked in layers one above the other (called a solera), each layer containing wine of a different year.

The youngest wine is at the top, the oldest on the bottom. As part of the oldest is removed (around one-third) to be fortified, sweetened and sometimes further matured in another solera, the space left is filled with wine from the next and younger layer above. That space is then filled in the same manner from the layer above it and so on until the space in the youngest cask at the top is filled with the new vintage's wine.

Sherries made by this most traditional and labour-intensive method are guaranteed a remarkable uniformity and are much prized. Unfortunately, the current decline in sherry sales puts this method at risk.

MUSCAT AND TOKAY

These two wines keep regular company generally because it is a difficult decision to choose one over the other, such is their similarity in richness and overall quality.

While many regions, notably Western Australia's Swan Valley and the Barossa Valley in South Australia, make some delightful styles of both, it must be said that their home is northeastern Victoria around Rutherglen, Glenrowan and Wahgunyah. This region produces unique, classical qualities unrivalled elsewhere in the world.

The warmth of the sun is a definite factor, with the grapes being left on the vine much longer than normal table-wine grapes to develop high sugar content. The grapes for muscat and tokay — muscat à petits grains and muscadelle (also called tokay) respectively — have quite strong individual qualities that, after the addition of a fortifying spirit, are heightened by cask maturation.

Casks allow air into the wine as well as imparting warm, mellow flavours. Then the wine is ready for blending. Blends of younger material are used for wines more commercially priced, while the art of the blender is an important guarantee of the quality of the better wines. The older the material the better. As with most fortifieds, the winemaker blends a final product from wines from different years aiming for a balance of warm luscious flavours (not too sweet or cloying), a firm acid structure and a long, lingering finish. Individual years, no matter how exceptional the wine, can only ever be a base for these wines.

Makers like Morris and Baileys in northeastern Victoria are fortunate enough through good planning to be able to work with base wines as old as 40 to 80 years. They simply 'freshen' these up with younger wines (at least, young by their standards).

If a major difference can be defined between muscat and tokay, muscat is seen as being sweeter, more intense in flavour and it has become more in demand.

MADEIRA

Verdelho grapes were originally brought to Western Australia from the small Atlantic island of Madeira to make this famous dessert wine, which is fermented and aged in wood. As the demand for madeira dropped, the grapes were used to make an appealing table wine.

Some good examples of Australian madeira still exist and are noticeable for their rich golden colours with hints of honey and spice.

VERMOUTH

This well-known mixer falls into three categories – sweet, medium and dry. Full-bodied grape varieties are the basis of the sweet style; light dry grapes are the basis of the latter two styles.

The process is quite simple with one interesting twist, the wines are blended and matured for a couple of years during which a sweetening agent is added. In the meantime, with a recipe most jealously guarded, the winemaker infuses a mixture of herbs and spices, such as angelica, bitter orange peel, camomile, peppermint, cinnamon, nutmeg, cloves, among others, in wine or spirit, which is then filtered and added to the base wine. It is then fortified.

All this is quite a lot of work for something that has fallen out of fashion, but big companies like Angove's with its Marko brand continue to reap reasonable returns.

BRANDY

Australian brandy has enjoyed a mixed history since the first stills were imported in 1807, with makers suffering the perils of Prohibitionists and restrictive tax policies. The latter, an excise tax, is in large part responsible for the industry's steadying decline. Despite all that, quality remains very high and prices for some older brandies can still be considered bargains.

Brandy is basically distilled white wine. Grapes should be neutral in flavour and dry like doradillo, palomino, pedro ximinez and trebbiano, and fermentation should be cool to retain their delicate nature.

The best brandies are made by the old-fashioned 'pot still' process in which the wine is placed in the lower section, heated to boiling point and the vapours rise to become trapped and condensed in the upper receiver. The vapour is drawn off until enough is collected to undergo a second distillation towards the end of which higher alcohols (important to bouquet and flavour) are given off. Now rated around 74 to 83 per cent alcohol, the brew is ready to be reduced in strength by the addition of distilled water and it is matured in oak casks for a minimum of two years to smooth and soften.

Older brandies are blends of various years and take on a number of initials or stars to indicate their basic age:

- one star = three years old (when bottled)
- two stars = four years old (when bottled)
- three stars = five years old (when bottled).

For liqueured brandies:
- VSO (Very Superior Old) = around 12 to 17 years old
- VSOP (Very Superior Old Pale) = 18 to 25 years old
- VVSOP or XO (Very, Very Superior Old Pale or Extra Old) = 25 to 40 years old.

And now to taste
The following is a selection of Australian fortified wines.

$$$

- **Campbells Liquid Gold Tokay**
  Cold tea is the taste you want from the muscadelle grape, known under its more glamorous name, tokay. It is delivered here in a classic north-east style, but it is just one of the many complexing factors – toffee, honey, caramel – in this remarkable wine.
- **Mountadam Ratafia Pinot Noir**
  Ratafia is basically a French-style apéritif, a blend of grape juice and brandy. It actually tastes better than it sounds, especially from an enthusiast like Mountadam, which changes the grapes used from year to year, mood to mood. The pinot noir exudes strawberries. Serve chilled and/or with ice.
- **Penfolds Magill Bluestone Tawny**
  In 1996 Penfolds released a new tawny into an already impressive fortified collection. The name is a reference

to the historic winery buildings used by the founder of Penfolds. The wine is tawny-red in colour and nutty in aroma with a fruit cake complexity of fruit, clean spirit and sweet oak.

- **Seppelt Viva 1 Liqueur Shiraz**
  Before Viva came along in 1995, the grapes for this stylish apéritif were earmarked for sparkling shiraz. Such is the calibre of fruit being used. This is no plaything, it is seriously intense with sweet, spicy flavours and deliciously clean spirit. Enjoy over ice as an apéritif.
- **Yalumba Ten Year Old Premium Port**
  The 'Ten' refers to the average age of this delightful tawny style, which, being lighter in bouquet and general mouthfeel, is modelled more on a Portuguese port. The dryness on the finish is an indicator of style too.

$$

- **Chateau Yaldara 15 Year Old Limited Edition Tawny Port**
  Belies its price with rich, mouthfilling flavour and aged characters from good blending. Delightful fruit cake complexity on the nose and typical tawny raisin sweetness. Yum.
- **Bethany White Port**
  The 'white' refers to the grape varieties used – muscadelle, frontignac, riesling – by this Barossa Valley maker to produce a simple, sweet fortified style that should probably

be served chilled for best effect. And no, it isn't exactly white in colour.

- **De Bortoli Liqueur Muscat 10 Year Old**
  Ten years sounds impressive until you realise some producers go back 70 years or more for blending material. This is not a criticism of what is a fresh, tasty wine from the Riverina that has a lasting flavour of dried fruit and clean spirit. Amazing for the price.

- **Hardy's Whiskers Blake Tawny Port**
  This is surely one of the most quaffable tawnies on the market today, with characteristic tawny sweetness and seductive dried fruit flavours coming through from start to finish. It is lighter in the mouth than many, almost tending towards Portuguese in style. Pleasantly clean and dry.

- **Scarpantoni Vintage Port 1991**
  From McLaren Vale with loads of lovely ripe fruit and intense flavour. Requires at least another five years, up to eight, to show its best.

$

- **Hardy's Tall Ships Tawny Port**
  A light, fruity style of tawny port supported by a sweet caramel flavour and well-rounded oak integration. Easy drinking style.

- **Morris Black Label Liqueur Muscat**

Barely comes in under $10 but is worth looking out for as a well-priced quality muscat from one of the great producers. Very sweet as you might expect but with real depth of flavour too.

- **McWilliam's Medium Dry Sherry**
  A classic, much-loved Australian style of sherry that is warm and spirity with a charming but noticeable sweetness. The secret to its success is a fresh, clean flavour that finishes quite dry.
- **Penfolds Club Port**
  A tried and true style that appeals to a wide cross-section of wine drinkers. Its sweet fruit and outstanding warm wood integration has resulted in a fortified wine of richness and long-lived flavour.
- **Yalumba Clocktower Tawny Port**
  It is difficult to find quality fortifieds below $10 a bottle but here is one from a respected Barossa Valley producer. A simple but highly quaffable sweet tawny.

Which food?

It is rare for fortified wines to be served throughout an entire meal, although some people have been known to have done just that. Most of us tend towards a more conservative approach to these very alcoholic wines.

Fortified wines tend to start and finish a meal, although it is very common to serve cheese with a fortified wine rather than with a full-bodied red and to serve some desserts with fortified styles.

Pre-dinner drinks Dry or medium dry sherry such as flor fino.

Hors d'oeuvre Grilled prawns are an ideal accompaniment to a fresh and lively dry fino sherry.

Soup Hot or cold consommé is fine with a medium dry sherry or amontillado sherry.

Dessert The traditional Christmas plum pudding just wouldn't be the same without an equally rich and smooth liqueur muscat, tokay or tawny port. A very sweet, rich dessert like pudding can easily take a fortified wine, and so, too, perhaps surprisingly, a chocolate dessert can take a liqueur muscat.

Cheese Rich cheeses like blue-vein, vintage cheddar, roquefort and blue wensleydale find good partners in most ports, muscats and tokays, and then there is stilton, which is always a delight accompanied by a port.

After-dinner drinks The classic spirits offered after a meal are liqueurs and brandies. There are the Australian liqueurs from the popular Baitz brand or the imported kind like the brandy-based Dom Benedictine, but a more than suitable replacement to aid the digestion is an old vintage port, tawny port, muscat or tokay.

THE LANGUAGE OF WINE

The following are definitions of many of the terms associated with the making and tasting of wine. Cross-references are indicated in italic type.

Acid: is naturally found in grapes and is present in wine in two main forms – tartaric and malic. Tartaric is highly desirable for its crisp sharpness and is permitted to be added to Australian wine in powdered form. Malic is an 'appley' hard acid that often needs to be softened by a secondary fermentation (*malolactic fermentation*).

Alcohol: alcohol in wine is produced by the action of *yeasts* on grape sugars during *fermentation*. Most table wine is between 11 and 14 per cent alcohol, and *fortifieds* are between 17 and 19 per cent.

Apéritif: the French term for an appetiser drink served before a meal. This can often be a sherry or a sparkling wine.

Appellation controlée: originally French and now adopted by many countries as a system of guaranteeing the authenticity of wine on the label by including its origin, grape varieties and sometimes methods of *viticulture* and winemaking.

Aroma: often used synonymously with '*bouquet*' but, strictly speaking, aroma relates to the smell of the grape (especially when young) while bouquet relates to the smell of the wine.

Aromatic: a tasting term for the smell of a wine, usually very floral and *spicy*.

Barrique: an oak barrel with 225-litre capacity. Popular size for ageing wine in France and now Australia.

Baumé: the French term used for measuring sugar content in grapes. One degree baumé equals approximately one per cent alcohol in finished wine.

Bead: the bubbles rising in a glass of sparkling wine. The smaller the bead the better the wine.

Bitter: is an unpleasant taste (and hence a fault) caused by excessive *tannin* extraction from the skin, pips and stalks of grapes.

Blackcurrant: an attractive smell and taste usually associated with cabernet sauvignon wine. Is also known as 'cassis'.

Body: the weight of wine in the mouth (light, medium, full) due to *alcohol* content and *tannin*.

Botrytis cinerea: the fungus that can infiltrate ripe grapes, shrivelling the outside, reducing the water content inside and concentrating sweetness and flavour to produce intense, honeyed wines. Also known as 'noble rot'.

Bouquet: a tasting term for the fragrance of wine, which comes not only from *fermentation* but, more importantly, bottle maturation.

Breathing: a method of allowing the wine to come in contact with air before serving (can include decanting, see *Decant*), which can sometimes remove 'off' odours and improve *bouquet*.

Brut: the French term describing the driest style of champagne or sparkling wine.

Burnt rubber: an unattractive wine smell that can spoil enjoyment. See *Mercaptan*.

Capsule: the covering around the neck of a wine bottle that protects the cork. The use of lead capsules has been phased out in Australia; aluminium, plastic and composite varieties have replaced the toxic lead capsule.

Carbonated wine: a relatively cheap sparkling wine made by the injection of carbon dioxide to provide the bubble.

Carbonic maceration: an age-old winemaking technique

using whole, uncrushed grape bunches. Also a registered wine name, Cab Mac, made by the Mitchelton wine company in Victoria and using similar techniques.

Charmat: the method invented by the French of making economical sparkling wine in bulk in large pressure tanks.

Cloudy: an unattractive feature in wine showing suspended particles and obscuring colour.

Cloying: excessively sweet with insufficient *acid* to balance wine; unattractive.

Coarse: characterised by *hard* acidic taste with bitterness. A winemaking fault.

Complex: a tasting term for a highly desirable smell and taste depicting many different nuances.

Corked: an 'off' flavour in wine (mouldy, sour) produced by a defective cork.

Crust: the sediment often found in older red wines and *fortifieds* containing harmless natural by-products (tartrate crystals) from the wine's development.

Decant: a method of allowing the wine to come in contact with air (see *Breathe*) or removing its sediment by pouring the contents of a bottle into a carafe or decanter.

Demi-sec: a champagne term indicating wine that is medium sweet or semi-dry.

Digestif: the French term for an after-dinner drink.

Dry: Wine in which the sugar has been fermented right out, indicating lack of sweetness.

Earthy: a tasting term to describe a smell or taste of the soil. This is often associated with wine from warmer wine regions.

Esters: a reaction of *acid* with *alcohol* that gives a smell of acetone or nail polish to a wine. Highly *volatile* in big amounts.

Extractive: an unattractive and *coarse* feature of a wine from heavy-handed extraction of juice from skins and pips; mouth puckering.

Fermentation: the age-old process of turning grapes into wine by the action of *yeasts* (naturally found on the grapes or added) on the grape sugars, which converts into alcohol and carbon dioxide.

Filtering: removes solids (*lees*, *fining* residues, impurities) from wine to produce clean, bright wines. However, heavy filtering can remove precious flavour components.

Fining: the gentle clarifying of the wine before it is bottled, often by the use of egg whites.

Flabby: too many ripe fruit characters with insufficient acid.

Fortified: wines that have had alcohol (grape spirit, brandy spirit) added during making, for example, port, sherry, tokay, muscat.

Free-run: generally regarded as the best quality juice for wine; it is the first juice to flow freely from the grape in the crusher on arrival at the winery.

Garlic: an unattractive smell that can spoil enjoyment. See *Mercaptan*.

Green: a tasting term that applies to young wine that is unbalanced because of excessive *acid* and use of immature grapes.

Hard: too much *tannin* and/or *acid* in wine, which brings bitterness.

Herbaceous: a tasting term to describe grassy or herbal flavours and smells, most notable in sauvignon blanc and cabernet sauvignon.

Hogshead: a wooden barrel of 300-litre capacity for storing and imparting oak flavour to a wine.

Hydrogen sulphide (H_2S): the smell of rotten eggs in wine, a fault caused by bad winemaking or storage.

Jammy: a tasting term for red wine generally from very warm to hot areas with sweet, jam-like features – often *cloying* and unpleasant.

Late-picked: grapes picked later (and therefore riper) than usual to increase sugar levels and produce wines spätlese or auslese in style.

Lees: the sediment found on the bottom of wine containers (bottle, oak cask) during the life of a wine. Can also be part of the winemaking process in which wine rests on its lees to produce *complex*, full flavours. The term 'sur-lee' found on some bottles, especially German and French wines, indicates that the wine was bottled straight out of the barrel. In champagne and sparkling wine it gives a yeasty flavour.

Legs: the columns of wine that remain on the inside of the glass after the wine has been drunk. Supposed to be a good sign as well as indicating high alcohol in a wine.

Length: the longer the flavour in the mouth after tasting, the better the wine; for example, 'good length'.

Madeirised: flavour component in some older wines (whites and *fortifieds*) following *oxidation* with a sweet almond-like flavour; can be attractive depending on degree.

Malolactic fermentation: the winemaking term for secondary fermentation converting 'green apple' malic *acid* into softer, more complex lactic acid. Common in red and, increasingly, white winemaking.

Mercaptan: a sour, unpleasant smell (burnt rubber and garlic are most common) due to the breakdown of hydrogen sulphide.

Méthode champenoise: the original French method of making sparkling wine in which the wine undergoes secondary *fermentation* in the bottle in which it is to be sold.

Must: unfermented grape juice.

Noble rot: a synonym for *Botrytis cinerea*.

Nutty: a pleasant smell usually found in sherry and associated with wood maturation and bottle development.

Oak: a favourite means of storing wine (mainly reds and some whites like chardonnay and sauvignon blanc) to impart extra dimension and complex flavours. French, American and German oak are highly favoured.

Oenology: the science of winemaking.

Oloroso: the Spanish term for old, rich, sweet sherry.

Oxidation: the effect of air on wine (notably through bad corks) with a resulting loss of flavour and palatability.

pH: an expression of a wine's acidity (in relation to its alkalinity). Most Australian wines have pH values of between three and four, with the lower the pH the better the ageing ability.

Phylloxera: a devastating vine insect that destroyed European and Australian vineyards late last century. American rootstocks are resistant and are now used extensively. This pest is still present in some areas but is kept under control.

Pressings: the term for wine after pressure is applied to release extra juice from skins, seeds and pulp of the grapes (to provide a more tannic wine).

Puncheon: a large oak barrel of around 500-litre capacity.

Racking: transferring wine from one cask or barrel to another to draw wine off *lees*.

Rancio: highly attractive and distinctive developed wood character in old dessert wines, the result of oxidation. Can be quite *nutty* in taste.

Residual sugar: grape sugar left in wine after *fermentation*. Gives a degree of sweetness to a wine – the more sugar left, the sweeter the taste.

Smoky: a character given off from oak barrels that are fired or charred to bend them into shape during their making.

Solids: the suspended particles of skin and flesh in grape juice. If not removed before *fermentation* they can contribute coarse characters.

Spice: the attractive aromatic characters on the nose and palate akin to spices.

Stalky: the bitter characters derived from contact with the grape stalks during winemaking.

Sulphur dioxide (SO_2): a winemaker's most common tool used to prevent *oxidation* and as a preservative. Too much can result in undesirable odours.

Tannin: an essential preservative derived from grape skins during *fermentation*. In young wine (mostly red) can be bitter but necessary for longevity. Oak barrels also contribute tannin to a wine.

Tart: a sharp-tasting sensation due to too much acidity or *tannin*.

Tartaric acid: the principal acid in grapes, contributing to a wine's quality and crisp finish.

Toasty: a tasting term for the smell of freshly toasted bread usually derived from barrel *fermentation* or maturation or bottle age.

Ullage: in a bottle of wine, the space between the cork and the wine. Not terribly important unless the wine is below the neck of the bottle (generally in older wines), which may indicate spoilage.

Varietal: can be a term for wine made entirely from a single grape variety or at least dominated by that variety, or the distinctive smell and taste of particular grape varieties.

Vintage: can be the time of year the grapes are picked or harvested, or the year (which appears on the label) in which a wine was made.

Viticulture: the growing and maintenance of grape vines.

Volatile: often indicates the first step towards deterioration by the presence of acetic *acid* (vinegary smell, sharp taste).

Yeast: the organisms that help to convert the sugar inside grapes into *alcohol* during *fermentation*.

WINE REGIONS

NEW SOUTH WALES

Lower Hunter Valley

The Hunter Valley is divided into Lower and Upper not only geographically but historically. The Lower (the Cessnock–Pokolbin area) is the hub of activity and among Australia's oldest existing wine regions, where early pioneers Lindemans and McWilliam's Mount Pleasant made their mark. Latter-day pioneers Tyrrell's, Rothbury Estate and Lake's Folly continue a long and proud tradition built largely on the fortunes of two grapes – semillon and shiraz – but that increasingly includes chardonnay and cabernet sauvignon.

- **Best vintages of the last decade:** 1987, 1988 (whites), 1989, 1990 (reds), 1991, 1993 (whites), 1994 (whites), 1995, 1996 (whites).
- **Exceptional years:** 1991 (reds), 1993 (whites), 1995 (whites).
- **Recommended vineyard tours–tastings:** Broken-wood, Allandale, Parker Wines, Tyrrells, Lake's Folly, Rothbury Estate.

Upper Hunter Valley

If the Lower Hunter has a crowded, colourful history, the

Upper Hunter has the modern winemaker's dream – space.
A desire to expand saw Penfolds open up the area centring
on Muswellbrook in the 1960s. A number of smaller vineyards
followed but the two that have made the most of the
sometimes difficult conditions (including, as surprising as it
may seem, soils too rich for some vines) are Rosemount
Estate and Arrowfield. Both have enjoyed tremendous success
with their white wines, notably Rosemount with its chardonnay.
Rosemount's Roxburgh chardonnay was an early pioneer of
the full-flavoured buttery Australian style. (Rosemount has
also been expanding into other areas, notably Coonawarra,
McLaren Vale and Orange.) In 1989, Arrowfield was bought
by a group headed by Nick Whitlam and in 1990, with an eye
on expansion and export, it came under the control of a
Japanese company. After a name change to Mountarrow and
the creation of a number of wine labels, the company has
now returned to being called Arrowfield and is concentrating
on a new streamlined range.

- **Best vintages of the last decade:**   1987, 1989, 1990,
  1991, 1993, 1995.
- **Exceptional years:**   1987 (whites), 1989, 1991 (reds),
  1995 (whites), 1996 (reds).
- **Recommended vineyard tours–tastings:**   Rosemount
  Estate, Reynold's Yarraman, Arrowfield.

Mudgee
Despite a history as old as its neighbour, the Hunter Valley,
Mudgee remains a quiet backwater on the Australian wine

scene. A host of small vineyards, as yet without the quantities for any lasting national exposure, is dominated by the huge Montrose–Craigmoor–Amberton group that was taken over by Orlando in early 1989.

Both red and white wines do well in the lush hilly region with some excellent chardonnay and semillon being produced. Shiraz dominates the red wines.

An early convert to organic viticulture was Gil Wahlquist of Botobolar who influenced many others both inside and outside the district before his retirement to Sydney in 1994. New owners, Kevin and Trina Karstrom, have continued the Wahlquist philosophy. Equally controversial was the early establishment of an appellation control system to ensure that Mudgee grown and made wine is true to label and free from faults.

- **Best vintages of the last decade:**   1989, 1990, 1991, 1993, 1995, 1996.
- **Exceptional years:**   1991 (reds).
- **Recommended vineyard tours–tastings:**   Montrose, Botobolar, Miramar Wines, Thistle Hill.

Riverina

The Riverina's hot, arid climate made it the perfect place for fortified wine production, which is how it came to be established alongside the citrus fruit, rice and wheat industries of the soldier settlers of the 1920s. The area was originally known as the Murrumbidgee Irrigation Area (the MIA), but now prefers to be called the Riverina.

The McWilliam family company made its hugely successful cream sherry and fortified wines from the area. As tastes changed, the necessary move into table-wine production was a more challenging experience given the hot conditions. Today, the region's winemakers have all but conquered the inhospitable climate with extensive irrigation and are among the nation's biggest growers of wine grapes. The area is planted principally with white grape varieties that are produced mainly for the cask market.

- **Best vintages of the last decade:**   1987, 1988, 1990, 1991, 1994, 1995, 1996.
- **Exceptional years:**   1991, 1994, 1996 (whites).
- **Recommended vineyard tours–tastings:**   De Bortoli, Lilly Pilly Estate, Wilton Estate.

Australian Capital Territory

Canberra and district

This small and relatively new viticultural area is commonly referred to as the Canberra region, yet few vineyards can be found inside the boundaries of the Australian Capital Territory. The Yass Valley, as it is increasingly called, actually hosted a small wine industry in the 1860s, with the last winery finally succumbing to outside competition in 1908.

The rapid expansion of Canberra as our political centre in the 1950s and 1960s brought people with the desire and the money to invest. Consequently, the first of the 'new' vineyards were planted in the early 1970s. Professional people, especially former CSIRO staff, dot the vineyard landscape, among the most notable of whom was the former Governor of Victoria, the late Sir Brian Murray of Doonkuna Estate at Murrumbateman. Vineyard size and quantities remain small, which means the wines of Canberra–Yass Valley are not generally seen outside the area. A cool-climate region, there has been much experimentation in the past 15 years that should prove fruitful in the future, particularly with German-style aromatic whites as well as chardonnay and cabernet sauvignon. A number of vignerons are also hopeful it will become known as a sparkling wine region.

- **Best vintages of the last decade:** 1987, 1988, 1990 (whites), 1991, 1993, 1995.
- **Exceptional years:** 1991, 1995 (whites).
- **Recommended vineyard tours–tastings:** Lark Hill (Bungendore), Clonakilla (Murrumbateman), Doonkuna Estate (Murrumbateman), Helm's Wines (Murrumbateman).

VICTORIA

Bendigo and district

Like so many Victorian wine areas, the history of the Bendigo region can be divided into pre- and post-phylloxera, phylloxera being a particularly destructive insect that first visited Victoria in the late nineteenth century. It destroyed Bendigo's flourishing wine industry set up in the wake of the gold rush and it is only relatively recently that vineyards have returned.

The year 1969 saw Bendigo pharmacist Stuart Anderson

establish Balgownie at Maiden Gully, and with a host of magnificent red wines it immediately attracted others. Cabernet sauvignon and shiraz tend to dominate, producing intense minty flavours in the former and incredible spicy richness in the latter. While Stuart Anderson was later to sell out to Mildara Blass, there have been others, equally enthusiastic, to take his place.

- **Best vintages of the last decade:** 1987, 1988, 1989, 1990, 1991, 1992, 1995, 1996.
- **Exceptional years:** 1989 (whites), 1992.
- **Recommended vineyard tours–tastings:** Water Wheel Vineyard, Blackjack (Harcourt), Passing Clouds, Jasper Hill.

Geelong

One of Melbourne's closest wine areas has a glorious, if tragic, history. Swiss immigrants were attracted to the area in the mid 1800s and immediately set to developing vineyards that were to eventually make Geelong the most important wine-growing area in the young State. Then phylloxera struck.

As a result of this rampant insect – the vine's most deadly enemy – every vineyard was destroyed. More than 100 years later, the region has yet to achieve the level of plantings of that golden era. Quality suffers no such problem, however, with pinot noir, cabernet sauvignon and chardonnay doing well in the cool climate.

- **Best vintages of the last decade:** 1987, 1988, 1989, 1991, 1992.

- **Exceptional years:** 1987 (reds), 1988, 1991.
- **Recommended vineyard tours–tastings:** Idyll Vineyard, Innisfail Vineyard (Batesford), Scotchmans Hill.

Gippsland

It is common to describe Gippsland as 'new' to Australian winemaking when in fact it was producing wine back in the nineteenth century. The misconception has been aided by the fact that the early industry failed to make any lasting impact, and the area is more noted today for its coal and coastal resorts. A small group of winemakers hopes to change all that with a range of fine wines, predominantly red.

Experimentation with pinot noir, cabernet sauvignon and its relatives cabernet franc and merlot has been very pleasing. At least one long-term producer, Nicholson River Winery, has joined the ranks as one of Victoria's best chardonnay makers with a highly flavoursome and intense style of wine.

- **Best vintages of the last decade:** 1987, 1988, 1989 (reds), 1991, 1993.
- **Exceptional years:** 1988, 1991.
- **Recommended vineyard tours–tastings:** The McAlister (by appointment), Nicholson River Winery, Wyanga Park.

Goulburn Valley

Traditionally, the Goulburn Valley has centred around Seymour and the neighbouring Nagambie wineries of Chateau Tahbilk and Mitchelton. However, today that area is better known as the Central Goulburn Valley, while isolated wineries like Tisdall at Echuca, Delatite at Mansfield and Plunkett's in the Strathbogie Ranges extend not only the Valley's boundaries but its recognised wine styles. Tisdall (with its successful chardonnay), Delatite (with its mastery of gewürztraminer and sauvignon blanc) and Plunkett's (with its crisp whites and full-bodied reds) complete the region's reputation as an all-rounder. Chateau Tahbilk and Mitchelton are also firm believers in the little-known French grape marsanne, with production of the white wine rivalling France.

- **Best vintages of the last decade:** 1987, 1988, 1990, 1991, 1992, 1993 (whites), 1994, 1995.
- **Exceptional years:** 1991, 1995 (reds).
- **Recommended vineyard tours–tastings:** Chateau Tahbilk, Plunkett's, Delatite, David Traeger Wines, Mitchelton.

The Grampians (formerly Great Western)

The story of Great Western is initially one of gold, and in its wake, the rise of a celebrated sparkling wine industry. In the 1890s businessman Hans Irvine brought out French equipment and champagne makers. It was he who planted ondenc, the white grape around which the industry was to flourish. In 1918 he sold out to Seppelt and the tradition continued to grow but was not exclusive to sparkling wine. Arawatta riesling, Moyston claret and Chalambar burgundy were highly successful table wines, as were those from fellow pioneers the Thomson family at Best's.

Today, Seppelt and Best's head a flourishing wine region

noted for exceptionally high standards of quality wine. And since the town of Great Western is just one of many, including Ararat and Hall's Gap, that lie on the winemaking trail, it was recently decided to change the region's official name to The Grampians.

- **Best vintages of the last decade:** 1988, 1990, 1991, 1992, 1994 (reds), 1995, 1996.
- **Exceptional years:** 1988, 1990, 1991 (reds), 1992, 1995 (reds).
- **Recommended vineyard tours–tastings:** Best's, Garden Gully, Montara, Mount Langi Ghiran, Seppelt Great Western.

Macedon

Macedon is the collective term for three wine-growing districts – Sunbury, Mount Macedon and Kyneton – that are each very different but have been somehow drawn together over time. Sunbury, the closest to Melbourne, has the longest viticultural association with present-day vineyards Craiglee and Goona Warra enjoying a long, if broken, history dating back to the 1860s.

Kyneton and Mount Macedon, among the fastest growing and coldest wine areas in Australia, owe their start to restaurateur Tom Lazar who established Virgin Hills in the late 1960s.

Kyneton is responsible for magnificent, deep-coloured, flavoursome cabernets while Mount Macedon is a most promising sparkling wine area.

- **Best vintages of the last decade:** 1987 (whites), 1988 (reds), 1990, 1991, 1993.
- **Exceptional years:** 1988 (reds), 1990 (reds), 1991.
- **Recommended vineyard tours–tastings:** Hanging Rock Winery, Knight's Granite Hills, Craiglee, Goona Warra, Romsey Vineyard.

Mornington Peninsula

Centred around the seaside resorts of Dromana and Merricks, the Mornington Peninsula has blossomed in the last decade or so both in size and reputation following a somewhat sluggish beginning. Its late start was no doubt due in part to the uncertainty of its suitability to grow grapes, strong winds whipped up from Port Phillip and Westernport bays producing gusty, cool growing conditions.

While Melbourne wine merchant Doug Seabrook was among the first to make wine on the Peninsula, it was retailer Baillieu Myer who established the first permanent winemaking operation at Elgee Park. That was in the 1970s. Today there are more than 36 wineries and 150 vineyards in the region concentrating on the production of quality table wines.

- **Best vintages of the last decade:** 1988, 1989 (whites), 1990, 1991, 1993, 1994, 1996 (whites).
- **Exceptional vintages:** 1988, 1991, 1993.
- **Recommended vineyard tours–tastings:** Dromana Estate, Karina Vineyard, Main Ridge Estate, Merricks Estate, Stonier's Winery, Tuck's Ridge Vineyard.

Murray Valley

The Murray Valley has the distinction of providing the Australian wine industry with a sizeable quota of its bulk and commercial wines. Sadly, it receives little recognition in return.

The hot, dry climate that makes irrigation essential is seen as the enemy of premium wines (irrigation is accused of pumping the grapes with water and diluting fruit flavour). This is strongly denied by those producers who, with care, have had success in recent years with a number of premium grape varieties, particularly chardonnay. It is not impossible to produce good wines from the area, which centres on Mildura and Robinvale, and those regularly making the extra effort are Alambie Wines, Best's St Andrews and Buller's. There is also no denying that the obvious economics of making good, cheap wines in the region has seen major companies establishing very large winemaking 'plants' – notably Mildara, McWilliam's and Lindemans.

- **Best vintages of the last decade:** 1988, 1989, 1991, 1993, 1995.
- **Exceptional years:** 1988, 1989 (whites), 1991, 1993, 1995 (whites).
- **Recommended vineyard tours–tastings:** Buller's, Lindemans Karadoc, Mildara, McWilliam's Robinvale.

Northeastern Victoria

The fame and fortune of this area has been built on the production of sweet, luscious fortified wines the likes of tokay, muscat, port and sherry. Generations of family fortified winemakers – Chambers, Morris, Brown, Campbell, Sutherland-Smith – have also become part of the region's enduring folklore. It all started around the time of the discovery of gold and the opening of export markets to London. Cycles of boom and bust followed but the magic of northeastern Victoria's fortifieds, centred on the towns of Rutherglen and Glenrowan, have endured because of their obvious superior, world-class quality.

Production of big, robust reds and, increasingly, quality white wines including sparkling now complete an extraordinary range of wine styles.

- **Best vintages of the last decade:**   1987 (reds), 1988, 1990, 1991, 1992, 1994 (whites), 1996.
- **Exceptional years:**   1988, 1991, 1994 (whites).
- **Recommended vineyard tours–tastings:**   All Saints, Bailey's, Brown Brothers, Chambers Rosewood, Morris, Stanton & Killeen.

Pyrenees

Although still widely known as the Avoca wine district, the Pyrenees is its more common name, coming from the area's attractive series of ranges. Its early history appears to have been dominated by the Mackereth family who in turn were overpowered by their more productive neighbours at nearby Great Western.

It was a joint venture between Remy Martin of France and a Melbourne wine merchant (Nathan and Wyeth) establishing Chateau Remy in the 1960s (now called Blue Pyrenees Estate) that attracted further investment in the area.

A producer of distinctly minty, solid red wines, the Pyrenees is now firmly established as a sparkling wine region (led by Taltarni and Blue Pyrenees Estate) and has a growing reputation for whites.

- **Best vintages of the last decade:** 1987 (whites), 1988, 1989, 1990, 1991, 1992, 1994 (reds), 1995, 1996.
- **Exceptional years:** 1988 (reds), 1990, 1991, 1994 (reds).
- **Recommended vineyard tours–tastings:** Blue Pyrenees Estate, Dalwhinnie, Taltarni, Mount Avoca Vineyard, Warrenmang.

Yarra Valley

It was Sophie de Montmollin (who was married to Victoria's Governor La Trobe) who played an important part in the establishment of the Yarra Valley as a grape-growing area. She encouraged Swiss viticulturists to immigrate (among them the de Castella brothers of St Huberts fame) who would lay the foundations for a most successful industry.

Faltering in the late nineteenth century, the wine industry was revived in the early 1970s by a band of enthusiasts led by doctors Peter McMahon and John Middleton. St Huberts, too, gained a second lease of life under the Cester family in the 1970s, but by 1996 had undergone three ownership changes (formerly part of the Rothbury Group, it is now owned by Foster's Mildara Blass). The Valley has also attracted considerable outside investment, first from the French champagne company Moët & Chandon, which has built a spectacular sparkling wine facility at Coldstream called Domaine

Chandon. Then in 1989 the De Bortoli family from Griffith opened its large restaurant and winery complex at what was once Chateau Yarrinya at Dixons Creek.

In recent years the landscape has changed dramatically with the arrival of major wine companies. Mildara Blass (now owned by Foster's) purchased young up-and-comer Yarra Ridge, BRL Hardy took over Yarra Burn and put in major plantings at Hoddles Creek, and Orlando Wyndham bought an established grower's vineyard. In 1996 the Champagne house Devaux entered into an agreement with Yering Station to produce Yarrabank sparkling wine and Coldstream Hills became part of Southcorp.

Despite a variety of soils and mesoclimates in the Valley, chardonnay and cabernet sauvignon are consistently elegant, while pinot noir is proving an exciting addition.

- **Best vintages of the last decade:**   1987, 1988 (reds), 1990, 1991, 1993 (reds), 1994.
- **Exceptional years:**   1987 (reds), 1990, 1991, 1993 (reds), 1994.
- **Recommended vineyard tours–tastings:**   Domaine Chandon, Yarra Ridge, Eyton on Yarra, De Bortoli, Oakridge, Yering Station.

SOUTH AUSTRALIA

Adelaide Hills
An ever-expanding region close to Adelaide, the Hills now incorporates parts of what would have previously been

regarded as the Barossa Valley, notably Eden Valley, Mount Pleasant and Keyneton. The effect of these hills and valleys is to provide a cool sheltered area eminently suitable for quality wine production.

The Eden Valley and environs is rightly regarded as one of Australia's greatest riesling producers. Keyneton, home to Henschke wines, is dominated by full-bodied cabernet sauvignon and shiraz. The newer Piccadilly area, settled early on by the enigmatic Brian Croser of Petaluma, is most sympathetic to chardonnay and pinot noir and, by association, sparkling wine.

- **Best vintages of the last decade:**   1987, 1988, 1989, 1990, 1991, 1993 (reds), 1994, 1995, 1996 (whites).
- **Exceptional years:**   1987 (whites), 1988 (reds), 1991, 1993 (reds), 1994 (reds), 1995 (whites).
- **Recommended vineyard tours–tastings:**   Robert Hamilton & Son, Mountadam, Henschke, Bridgewater Mill.

Adelaide Plains

Vineyards vie with market gardens for space in this pleasantly warm and dry growing area on the outskirts of Adelaide. The connection is strongest with the Grilli family at Primo Estate, former market gardeners who have come a long way in a very short time since establishing vineyards at Virginia in 1973. Among the most innovative winemakers in Australia, the Grilli family uses a variety of techniques to produce wines of great subtlety including cabernet sauvignon, colombard and a deliciously rich botrytised riesling.

In 1999 Barossa Valley Estates, which despite the name is

located at Angle Vale, decided to go into partnership with
BRL Hardy to construct a winery in the Barossa Valley. The
company traditionally sources fruit from a number of wine
areas and will now call the Barossa Valley home.

- **Best vintages of the last decade:** 1987 (reds), 1988,
  1989 (whites), 1990, 1991, 1993, 1994.
- **Exceptional years:** 1988, 1991.
- **Recommended vineyard tours–tastings:** Primo
  Estate.

Barossa Valley

The Barossa Valley established South Australia's reputation
as *the* wine State. The oldest and arguably the most important
wine region quantity-wise, the Barossa was settled by German
Lutheran farmers in the 1840s. Hence, the profusion of
German names, architecture, food and wine styles that still
persist today.

Large family-run companies – Seppelt, Yalumba, Leo Buring,
Orlando and Penfolds – established lasting empires that are now
familiar bywords to most wine drinkers, although Robert Hill-
Smith at Yalumba is the last to keep family control. Four of Australia's biggest wine companies have headquarters in the Valley.
Recent major changes include the purchase of Wolf Blass Wines
by Mildara (1990), which then became Mildara Blass (taken over
by Foster's in 1996). Basedow was purchased by Grant Burge
(1993), who in turn sold the name but not the winery to the Hill
group of companies (owners of Marienberg).

With a great diversity of climate the region is capable of

growing a whole spectrum of wines with warm riesling, earthy shiraz, cabernet sauvignon and port styles dominating.

- **Best vintages of the last decade:** 1987, 1988, 1989, 1990, 1991, 1993 (reds), 1994, 1995, 1996.
- **Exceptional years:** 1987 (whites), 1988 (reds), 1991, 1994 (whites).
- **Recommended vineyard tours–tastings:** Basedow, Elderton, Orlando, Rockford, Seppeltsfield, St Hallett, Yalumba.

Clare Valley

Named after County Clare, Ireland, the town of Clare and the surrounding land north of the Barossa Valley is among the most picturesque wine country in Australia. Wine has shared the limelight with other pastoral pursuits from the very beginning in the 1840s. But as wheat and sheep went through regular cycles of boom and bust, wine steered a steady path led by the Stanley Wine Company.

Early on, the selection of riesling as the district's most suitable grape helped establish an Australia-wide reputation. Tim Knappstein of Enterprise Wines (now simply called Tim Knappstein Wines) pioneered sauvignon blanc, while Wendouree and Quelltaler (now owned by Mildara Blass and known under a variety of label names such as Black Opal, Eaglehawk and Annie's Lane) produced some of the best reds. They maintain a strong tradition today along with Mitchell, Skillogalee and Leasingham.

- **Best vintages of the last decade:** 1987, 1988, 1989, 1991, 1993, 1994, 1995, 1996 (whites).

- **Exceptional years:** 1987 (whites), 1988 (reds), 1991, 1993, 1996 (whites).
- **Recommended vineyard tours–tastings:** Skillogalee, Tim Knappstein Wines, Mitchell, Grosset, Wendouree, Sevenhill, Leasingham.

Coonawarra

Coonawarra with its famous terra rossa red soil has become well known not only in Australia but around the world for its marvellous, long-living red wines. The terra rossa itself, a strip of limestone soil overlying an extensive water reserve, emanates in an all too short northerly line from the town of Penola.

Many major Australian wine companies have established vineyards here – BRL Hardy, Orlando Wyndham, Mildara Blass and Southcorp Wines (through Penfolds, Lindemans and Wynns). Cabernet sauvignon and shiraz are king, but the area also makes some lovely sauvignon blanc (Katnook) and riesling (Wynns). Hollick Wines has had considerable success with its sparkling wine, but quantities will always be small.

In 1989 the family-run Brand's Laira winery was taken over by McWilliam's while Seppelt bought Hungerford Hill.

- **Best vintages of the last decade:** 1987 (reds), 1988, 1990, 1992 (whites), 1993, 1994, 1995 (whites).
- **Exceptional years:** 1990, 1992 (whites), 1993 (reds).
- **Recommended vineyard tours–tastings:** Bowen Estate, Hollick Wines, Katnook Estate, Mildara, Redman's, Wynns.

McLaren Vale

The history of McLaren Vale is the story of two Englishmen,
John Reynell and Thomas Hardy, who built wine empires that
dominated life around McLaren Vale for more than 100 years.
John Reynell, with vine cuttings from South Africa, was the
first vigneron in the area and actually gave Thomas Hardy his
big break. But it was Hardy and successive generations of his
family who were to survive the longest, buying Reynella in
1982.

Unfortunately, financial problems beset the Hardy Wine
Company in the early 1990s and in 1992 it was bought by
Berri–Renmano. Now called BRL Hardy, it is Australia's second
biggest wine producer in terms of quantity.

For a long time McLaren Vale was a maker of red wines
with peculiarly 'barnyard' bouquets, as well as fortifieds. In
the 1990s an injection of enthusiasm and money has seen
the resurgence of shiraz, grenache and chardonnay to the
top of the popularity ladder. The arrival of Mildara Blass on
the scene, with its takeover of Andrew Garrett Wines and
Ingoldby Wines, has brought change along with new, fashionable
wineries such as Tatachilla Wines, Fox Creek Wines and
Haselgrove.

- **Best vintages of the last decade:** 1987, 1988, 1989,
  1990, 1991, 1993 (reds), 1994 (reds), 1995, 1996.
- **Exceptional years:** 1989 (reds), 1991, 1994 (reds).
- **Recommended vineyard tours–tastings:** Chateau
  Reynella, Fox Creek Wines, Coriole, Tatachilla, d'Arenberg,
  Ingoldby, Wirra Wirra, Haselgrove.

Riverland

South Australia's major wine producer, the Riverland vineyards stretch the length of the winding Murray River between Renmark, Berri, Loxton and Waikerie in the northeast of the State near the Victorian border. Hot and dry, the region is planted with grapes that were initially suited to fortified production (especially brandy) and, latterly, bulk wine for the cask market.

Angove's at Renmark has become well known for its St Agnes brandy, Marko vermouth and Green Ginger Wine. In 1992 the Riverland's biggest company, Berri–Renmano, purchased the ailing Hardy wine company to become BRL Hardy, one of Australia's largest wine companies. The bulk-wine producer, with a core of some 500 wine growers in the Riverland, had been moving into premium table wine production in the late 1980s but surprised many at the time of the purchase with its boldness.

- **Best vintages of the last decade:** 1987, 1988, 1989 (whites), 1990, 1991, 1993, 1994, 1995, 1996.
- **Exceptional years:** 1988, 1989 (whites), 1991, 1993, 1996.
- **Recommended vineyard tours–tastings:** Angove's, Berri–Renmano.

WESTERN AUSTRALIA

Margaret River

Touted as the newest star on the Australian wine scene, Margaret River runs the length of Western Australia's most southwestern tip, benefiting greatly from the moderating influence of coastal winds. While wine was made as early as 1890, it was not until a rush of medicos came to the region in the 1960s that reputations were made. Big companies are now eyeing the region, Southcorp making the first move in 1997 buying Devil's Lair which was followed by BRL Hardy buying into Brookland Valley. Foremost as producers of some extraordinary cabernet sauvignons and/or chardonnays are Leeuwin Estate, Moss Wood, Vasse Felix and Cape Mentelle.

- **Best vintages of the last decade:**   1987, 1988, 1989 (reds), 1990, 1991, 1992, 1993, 1994, 1995 (whites), 1996.
- **Exceptional years:**   1987, 1988, 1990 (reds), 1991, 1993, 1995 (whites).
- **Recommended vineyard tours–tastings:**   Brookland Valley, Cape Mentelle, Cullen, Leeuwin Estate, Moss Wood (by appointment), Pierro, Vasse Felix.

Mount Barker–Frankland River

Mount Barker–Frankland River is a collective and rather dry title for a series of widespread vineyards dotted around Mount Barker, Frankland, Albany and Denmark. Since the first commercial wine was only made in the early 1970s it is of little surprise that companies like Alkoomi, Goundrey, Plantagenet and Shemarin have yet to become household names.

The region received Australia-wide attention when the late Robert Holmes a Court bought the Forest Hill Vineyard at Mount Barker (which was sold by Janet Holmes a Court in mid-1994 to two oil-industry businessmen) but more lasting fame will undoubtedly apply to the quality riesling, chardonnay and shiraz being produced. The large Swan Valley-based Houghton wine company (part of BRL Hardy) recognised the potential of the Frankland early on.

- **Best vintages of the last decade:**   1988 (whites), 1989, 1990, 1991, 1993, 1994, 1995.
- **Exceptional years:**   1989 (reds), 1991, 1994 (whites).
- **Recommended vineyard tours–tastings:**   Chatsfield Wines, Goundrey Wines, Jingalla, Plantagenet, Wignall's King River Vineyard.

South-West Coastal Plain

A wine-growing area close to Perth, the South-West Coastal Plain is near (and therefore somewhat under the spell of) the older, more exuberant Swan Valley. Among the early vineyards was Peel Estate, established in the 1970s on land originally belonging to Thomas Peel, son of Sir Robert Peel. Other 1970s pioneers were Dr Peter Pratten of Capel Vale, which is arguably one of the best-known vineyards in the area, and the late Barry Killerby, who set up Leschenault Wines. Under Anna Killerby and her winemaking husband, Matt Aldridge, the winery underwent a name change to Killerby Wines and had found a new forceful direction before the couple moved in 1997 to the Yarra Valley.

- **Best vintages of the last decade:**   1988, 1989 (reds), 1991, 1993, 1994 (whites), 1996 (whites).
- **Exceptional years:**   1989 (reds), 1991, 1994 (whites).

- **Recommended vineyard tours–tastings:** Capel Vale, Killerby Wines, Peel Estate.

Swan Valley

The Swan Valley is noted for two major distinctions: it being one of the hottest wine-growing regions in the world, and Houghton's famous white burgundy. The long-term success of many wine ventures (originally geared to the production of fortified wine) speaks volumes for the ability of the Valley's producers to overcome hostile growing conditions. Leading the way has been the Houghton wine company (part of BRL Hardy) and its quintessential Australian white wine, still a brand leader after almost 60 years.

Another major Swan Valley producer is Sandalford.

- **Best vintages of the last decade:** 1987, 1988 (reds), 1989, 1992, 1993 (reds), 1994 (whites), 1995 (whites).
- **Exceptional years:** 1991, 1994 (whites), 1995 (whites).
- **Recommended vineyard tours–tastings:** Houghton, Sandalford.

Tasmania

Derwent Valley

In southern Tasmania, where once the climate was 'officially' deemed unsuitable for grape growing, a small number of brave vignerons have proved the boffins wrong. Often referred to as the father of the modern-day Tasmanian wine industry, businessman Claudio Alcorso pioneered a vineyard – Moorilla

Estate – on the banks of the Derwent River, north of Hobart, back in 1960. It was ravaging birds and not the weather that proved the most costly, but hard work was rewarded, particularly with pinot noir, chardonnay and riesling. Unfortunately, the Alcorso family lost control of the winery, which has now passed onto a group of private investors.

Riesling, too, has been a successful component to Meadowbank's growing stature helped by the Hickinbotham family who made the wine in Victoria up until 1985.

- **Best vintages of the last decade:**   1988, 1989, 1991, 1992, 1993, 1995, 1996 (pinot noir).
- **Exceptional years:**   1988, 1989 (whites), 1991, 1996 (pinor noir).
- **Recommended vineyard tours–tastings:**   Moorilla Estate.

Pipers Brook

Pipers Brook Vineyard, among Tasmania's best-known vineyards, takes its name from the windswept Pipers Brook region north of Launceston. Owned by Australia's first doctor of philosophy in viticulture, Andrew Pirie, Pipers Brook now dominates the island's vineyard plantings. In the 1980s, the area's reputation for superb cool-climate chardonnays and pinot noir resulted in a joint venture between Heemskerk and a leading Champagne house, Louis Roederer, to produce a sparkling wine called Jansz. In 1994 Heemskerk and another local producer Rochcombe were bought by businessman Josef Chromy, but were sold again in 1998 to Pipers Brook Vineyard. In turn,

Pipers Brook Vineyard decided to sell the Jansz label to Yalumba, leaving it to concentrate on its own new sparklings. The area has also done exceptionally well with riesling.

- **Best vintages of the last decade:**   1988, 1991, 1992, 1994, 1996.
- **Exceptional years:**   1991.
- **Recommended vineyard tours–tastings:**   Pipers Brook, Dalrymple, Delamere, Heemskerk.

Tamar Valley

Also in the north of the State is the heavily populated (by Tasmanian standards) Tamar Valley. To the northwest of Launceston, the Valley has an ever-increasing number of vineyards, by far the biggest of any other Tasmanian region. However, the majority of the 11 established vineyards are small concerns such as Elmslie, McEwin's Vineyard, Marions Vineyard, Glengarry Vineyard and St Matthias. With only small quantities of wine being made distribution is mostly confined to within the State, although Marions Vineyard under wine-maker Marion Semmens, with its cabernet sauvignon and chardonnay, and St Matthias, with cabernet sauvignon, chardonnay and riesling, can generally be found and are of good quality.

A lot of future development is expected to take place here.

- **Best vintages of the last decade:**   1988, 1989, 1991, 1992, 1995, 1996 (pinot noir).
- **Exceptional years:**   1988, 1991, 1996 (pinor noir).

• **Recommended vineyard tours–tastings:** Marions Vineyard, St Matthias.

QUEENSLAND

The tropical climes of Queensland would seem to preclude the growing of quality table wine, but not so.

Successful wine operations have been established as far north as Cairns and as far west as Roma (512 kilometres west of Brisbane), although the majority tend to congregate around the cooler area of Stanthorpe to the south, near the New South Wales border. Almost a dozen vineyards make up the Stanthorpe wine region, which also goes under the name of Granite Belt. Noted for its high altitude and hilly terrain, the Granite Belt is quite cool in climate, significantly cooler than say the Hunter Valley, and has been compared with areas like the Pyrenees in Victoria and Margaret River in Western Australia.

The introduction of modern winemaking technology has seen quality improve quite dramatically, and for those with the quantity, sales outside Queensland have been steadily growing. The best known of the Granite Belt wineries is undoubtedly the Robinsons Family Vineyards, which produces an excellent 'cool-climate chardonnay' under an attractive hibiscus label.

Chardonnay, shiraz and cabernet sauvignon all offer a bright future.

- **Best vintages of the last decade:**   1987 (reds), 1989, 1990, 1991, 1993 (reds), 1995.
- **Exceptional years:**   1989, 1990 (whites), 1991, 1993 (reds).
- **Recommended vineyard tours–tastings:**   Robinsons Family Vineyards (Ballandean), Rumbalara (Rumbalara), Stone Ridge Vineyard (Glen Alpin), Winewood (Ballandean).

NORTHERN TERRITORY

Australia boasts vineyards in every State and Territory, even in the hottest and seemingly most inhospitable areas like the dead heart of the Red Centre.

Summer temperatures often hit the old Fahrenheit century (37.8°C) and kangaroos, rabbits and wild parrots are the vines' most persistent enemies, but despite the trials Chateau Hornsby outside Alice Springs continues to flourish.

Former Alice Springs pharmacist Denis Hornsby originally planted vines for his own enjoyment but by 1979 he was making commercial quantities, which have since found a good market with interstate and overseas visitors to the area. Drip irrigation is essential to coax respectable quantities of juice from his shiraz, cabernet sauvignon, semillon and riesling grapes, although he does admit to sometimes adding some South Australian wine to 'make up volume'.

Australia's Main Wine-growing Regions

The following key identifies the wine-growing regions found on the map on pages 132–133.

Western Australia
 1 Margaret River
 2 Mount Barker–Frankland River
 3 South-West Coastal Plain
 4 Swan Valley

Northern Territory
 5 Alice Springs

South Australia
 6 Adelaide Hills
 7 Adelaide Plains
 8 Barossa Valley
 9 Clare Valley
10 Coonawarra
11 McLaren Vale
12 Riverland

Queensland
13 Stanthorpe

New South Wales
14 Lower Hunter Valley

15 Upper Hunter Valley
16 Mudgee
17 Riverina
18 Canberra and district

Victoria
19 Bendigo and district
20 Geelong
21 Gippsland
22 Goulburn Valley
23 The Grampians
24 Macedon
25 Mornington Peninsula
26 Murray Valley
27 Northeastern Victoria
28 Pyrenees
29 Yarra Valley

Tasmania
30 Derwent Valley
31 Pipers Brook
32 Tamar Valley

Darwin

WESTERN
AUSTRALIA

NORTHERN
TERRITORY

Perth

4
3
1
2

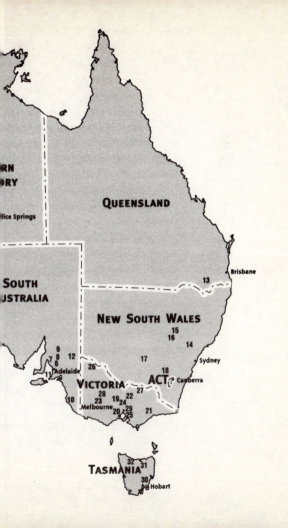